DUNCAN PRIDDLE knows Edinburgh's Royal Mile like the back of his hand. He's been up and down the Old Town closes and wynds more times than a seasoned street sweeper. His love affair wi[...]somed during his spell wit[...]alking tour company – Th[...]

Not content wi[...]lished tales, Duncan spen[...] dusty volumes in search o[...]rbelly. He then teamed up with his illiterate colleagues from The Cadies and Witchery Tours to share his passion for the Mile with a wider audience. Additional research was carried out by Brien Forbes and Lorna McWilliams. Gavin Wallace acted as editor. Robin Mitchell acted as a hindrance.

Lorna Baxter and Cameron Pirie pinned their revisionist colours to the literary mast by agreeing to co-ordinate the extensive updating programme. Robin Mitchell continued to act as a hindrance.

Duncan Priddle, now 33, no longer leads unsuspecting strangers down dark alleyways off the Royal Mile in the guise of a long-dead highway robber, and is engaged on a crusade to save the planet as a City of Edinburgh Countryside Ranger.

Robin Mitchell founded The Cadies and Witchery Tours in 1984, and became a member of the Scottish Tourist Guides Association in 1986. His first novel, *Grave Robbers*, was published in 1999. The Cadies and Witchery Tours recently celebrated its 15th gory year, despite Mitchell's continued involvement.

...th this historic highway blosso...
...th Edinburgh's award winning wa...
...e Cadies and Witchery Tours.
...th continually expounding estab...
...t many happy hours thumbing...
...the Royal Mile's anecdotal under...

Edinburgh's Historic Mile

DUNCAN PRIDDLE

Luath Press Limited

EDINBURGH

www.luath.co.uk

First published 1994 (Cadies Publishing)
Revised 2000

The paper used in this book is recyclable. It is made from low
chlorine pulps produced in a low energy, low emission manner
from renewable forests.

Printed and bound by
Omnia Books Ltd., Glasgow

Typeset in 10pt Sabon by S. Fairgrieve

Illustrations by
M. Thomson (pp 15, 16, 22, 33, 34, 38, 59, 60, 64, 73, 80)
and P. Bankhead (pp 19, 21, 44, 51, 57, 70, 74)

Cover design and Edinburgh Castle photograph by Tom Bee

The Palace of Holyroodhouse photograph © Queen Elizabeth II

Royal Mile map by Jim Lewis

Dedicated to all residents of, and visitors to,
Edinburgh's Royal Mile – past, present and future

Contents

Foreword

Edinburgh's Historic Mile is out and about at last! Not since the day of my public execution on 27 March 1811 in Edinburgh's Grassmarket can I remember an event so eagerly and excitedly awaited in the Old Town, and far beyond.

In the years that have passed since I led the first Witchery Murder and Mystery Tour, demand for my haunting nightly excursions around sinister Old Edinburgh has proved insatiable. The spell of the eerie closes and looming tenements, where the turbulent and sinister past of the city seeps from every stone, is potent indeed – if not addictive. The publication of my own *Witchery Tales* appears to have further whetted the appetite of citizen and tourist alike for the endless fascination and surprise which springs from the unique history of this ancient city, but I have long felt the need for a more comprehensive guide to its riches.

Here it is. It is a great honour to be associated with a book written and edited by my colleagues, the latter-day Cadies of Old Edinburgh. *Edinburgh's Historic Mile* is a wonderfully accurate and evocative guide to this most haunting of streets, which places the Royal Mile firmly at the heart of Old Edinburgh's story. With their familiar combination of erudition, enthusiasm and wit, the Cadies unfold in these pages a mile-long procession of all the wonder, terror and pride that marches down this thoroughfare through a nation's past, not forgetting to mention some of the sillier and decidedly surreal side-streets of Edinburgh's history along the way.

I am already indebted to this invaluable and unique compendium for a truly exhaustive trove of information, without which my walking tours would be infinitely poorer.

Whether you benefit from *Edinburgh's Historic Mile* as an intrepid explorer or a fascinated reader, I have no doubt that like countless other citizens and visitors, you will soon have cause to be grateful that it was the Cadies who safely guided you throughout a remarkable journey.

Adam Lyal (Deceased)

Headpiece

EDINBURGH'S AND SCOTLAND'S best-known thoroughfare, the Royal Mile, has often been likened to the form of a fishbone. During the glacial period, ice forced its way over the adamantine Castle Rock and left huge deposits in its wake on the leeward side. On this inhospitable ridge, running gradually downwards and eastwards, evolved a medieval city connected to the head of Edinburgh Castle like a backbone, its three hundred or so closes and wynds running off on either side like smaller vertebrae for about a mile's length, down to the tail of the Palace of Holyroodhouse.

It is the aim of this book to provide a detailed, but manageable, guide to the infinite riches and secrets to be found in the astonishing extent of Edinburgh's historic way. *Edinburgh's Historic Mile* does not pretend to be comprehensive, nor is it a history of Old Edinburgh, or Scotland. Rather it is designed as both a walker's companion, and a fireside one. While acknowledging the Mile's most celebrated landmarks, stories and legends, this book is 'alternative' in that it includes lesser-known, frequently eccentric, always fascinating information of the kind which is usually erased from the grimly serious, and sweetly poetic, literature of this most written about of streets.

For the foot-slogging visitor: your journey begins at Edinburgh Castle and thence proceeds in an easterly direction. It is recommended that the Mile be explored in the comfortable sections represented by the chapter divisions, at the rate of a chapter per day. To attempt more would be to squander untold historical and architectural riches which deserve, and repay, respectful and leisurely contemplation.

To the interested reader: browse, peruse and study as you wish, though remember that the text will be even better appreciated in the presence of the real thing.

To walkers, readers, visitors, residents and all possible combinations thereof: this book is written in the spirit of the one-time 'guardians of the street' in 18th century Edinburgh, the Cadies, or messenger-boys. Famed for their encyclopaedic knowledge of the labyrinthine complexity of the Mile's warren of wynds and closes, they would escort visitors safely to their destinations; deliver messages or goods; provide invaluable information to anyone who asked. Living and sleeping on the streets like wretches and renowned for their cheek, they were also greatly trusted, and seldom unfaithful. It is believed that the Cadies' intimate knowledge of nearly everybody's business in the Town helped to account for a spectacularly low crime-rate for the times. In many ways, the extraordinarily energetic, democratic and dramatic character of life in Old Edinburgh found in the Cadies its ideal expression.

The following pages are written in their spirit. Had the means been at their disposal, they would surely have written a book too.

CHAPTER I

It's All Downhill from Here

ASSUMING YOU HAVE DECIDED not to visit Glasgow or stop
for an early lunch, our tour begins at the head of the Royal
Mile, where a majestic and austere edifice blocks any further progress. This is the carpark attendant, and the large
building behind him is, of course, **Edinburgh Castle** (w1)
itself.

A comprehensive tour of Scotland's most visited monument is beyond the scope of this volume, as it would be
vain to compete with the acres of print which have been
devoted to every stone of this most Scottish of Valhallas.
A few of its major features, however, are worth dwelling on.
Situated some 440 feet above sea level and bordered on
three sides by volcanic cliffs, a more dramatic or impreg-
nable fortress can scarcely be imagined. Or a more conve-
nient one. As the more perceptive among the many visitors
who file across the ramparts every year are often heard to
observe, it really was a stroke of genius to build the city's
castle so close to its railway station.

As you cross the drawbridge you will be scrutinised by
the two great national heroes of Scotland: William Wallace
and Robert the Bruce. As far as these two saviours of
national freedom are concerned, you can be as cheeky as
you like, because they're statues (worth mentioning, just in
case it isn't obvious). Much less obvious is the ironic fact
that both likenesses of our great defenders against the
encroachments of the Auld Enemy were cast in England in
1929 and that a Californian, Randall Wallace, was so
impressed by the statue of his namesake that he researched

his story and wrote the film without which the Scottish Parliament may not have happened – *Braveheart*, starring Mel Gibson, an Australian. The rest is history, or Holywood.

Though 'Edinburgh Castle' has now been reached, this extensive site comprises a combination of disparate buildings, functions and epochs. The earliest structure on the rock – and possibly in the whole city – is the Chapel of St Margaret, built by King David I atop a pinnacle in memory of his pious mother. It has survived the Castle's centuries-long cycle of wreck and repair to retain its air of sanctity from the thunder of guns, and those members of the Scottish Armed Forces suitably inspired can even arrange a wedding here.

If this information occasions a swift exit from the Chapel and you walk eighteen yards from the main door, you will fall over a cliff. The less lemming-like might prefer to stop at sixteen yards, peer down over the mighty defences, and behold an unorthodox monument to that world beyond life's bourne. Or rather, bone. This is a graveyard all right, but one reserved exclusively for the mortal remains of ex-regimental dogs who have shuffled off this mortal collar and, er, ceased to bark. Such faithful old snarling sergeants and military mutts as Scamp, Tinker and Yum-Yum are laid to tummy-rubbing rest here in a most fetching nose-to-tail manner.

Leaving the dogs' boneyard, the famous half-moon battery nearby, bedecked by cannons, commands the attention. Queen amongst the cannons, and in fact regally hidden from public view, is Mons Meg. This muckle iron murderer, acquired by James II in 1457, is of such a scale that several children are said to have been conceived within her icy gullet – followed by a shotgun wedding? Her majesty

 currently resides in the Castle vaults to protect her from the elements. In her heyday, Meg was capable of launching a 500lb cannonball over a distance of two miles. So laborious was the loading process, however, that she was capable of the feat no more than twice an hour.

The network of underground vaults in which Meg enjoys retirement are of an analogous scale, for they carry the fantastic weight of the Castle's enormous superstructure. The cellars have served several different uses. During the Napoleonic Wars, they incarcerated French prisoners of war, many of whom expressed sentiments relevant to their unfortunate situation in the form of 18th century Gallic graffiti preserved to this day ('Bonaparte is a bam', etc.). The Castle was for a long time the state prison.

From the labyrinthine chambers possibly spring the many popular myths concerning secret underground passageways. A certain Arthur Elrine of Ohio, USA, claimed that while he was stationed in the Castle during 1920–21, he walked down a dark tunnel which stretched from the Castle to the Palace of Holyroodhouse. Those interminable regimental dinners awash on oceans of port can do the strangest things. On the other hand, anyone who has traversed the length of the Royal Mile on a wet Sunday afternoon in November could tell Arthur Elrine of Ohio, USA, a thing or two about long, dingy tunnels.

Unless you've a few weeks to waste locating the entrance to Arthur's ghostly gallery, it might be more advisable to leave the Castle by the main entrance, unless you've brought your hang-glider, in which case your next port of call will be the Firth of Forth – not covered by this book. Ahead is the apparently featureless expanse of the Castle Esplanade, as devoid of interest as car parks or empty

venues for Military Tattoos and occasional rock-extravaganzas tend to be. There are of course majestic views to be had north and south, following which an eager eye might detect an unusual plaque right in the north-east corner of the car park, with a small ornate fountain beneath.

Constructed in 1894 and erected in 1912, this is one of few 20th century monuments to one of the more dismal achievements of Scottish history; the torturing, strangling and burning of over 4,000 men and women for suspected witchcraft throughout the country between 1479 and 1722. Some 300 of these wretched victims met their appalling end on or near the site marked by the **Witches' Well** (N1). The eccentric, the insane or merely the innocently dotty – perceived as a threat to a rigorously policed social order – were readily denounced as being in league with the Devil, and subjected to a trial which consisted almost exclusively of torture. Dooking, thumb-screws, spiked barrels, the branks, ankle-crushing, witch-pricking: these and equally savage methods of inflicting agony would take the victim to such unfathomable extremes of mental and physical distress that the almost banal denouement of being *worryit* – strangled and then burned at the stake – must have beckoned as a ghastly blessing.

The vast majority of the innocents executed on the

Castlehill were of course female, a fact which betrays a deep-running fear of femininity festering beneath the solidly male-controlled hierarchies of government and religion throughout Scotland's history and, many would argue, as much a blight in the present day. The atrocities symbolised by the Witches' Well have disappeared, though more insidious and subtle forms of discrimination have not.

The building to which the Well is attached was, at one time, the Castlehill reservoir. Constructed in the mid-19th century and with a capacity of 2 million gallons of Victorian bathwater, it might, ironically, have doubled neatly as a prime location for dooking suspected witches. Enthusiasts for Scotland's renowned legal system might pause to consider that a woman was tried for witchcraft in Tain just a few decades before this bastion of a squeaky-clean civilisation was erected. Today the building houses a Tartan Weaving Mill and Exhibition Centre where you can learn about every stage of manufacture and even weave tartan cloth by hand.

On the opposite side of the street, **Cannonball House** (s2) fills the view. By the curious interconnectedness of things, the building's origins and history have nothing whatsoever to do with projectiles, and everything to do with the tartan bathtub. The eponymous cannonball can be seen by walking six or seven steps down **Castle Wynd** (s1), and looking between the two largest windows on the west face of the house. Seemingly lodged in the facade is a spherical object which, contrary to popular belief, is neither a cannonball fired at advancing Jacobites in 1745, nor a resident's last desperate attempt to get rock group Texas to play a few thousand watts less deafeningly during their last Esplanade sell-out. The truth is woefully devoid of drama, and notoriety. The cannonball is a memorial marker indicating the maximum gravitational height of the reservoir's first piped water supply to the city. Quite why this immensely underwhelming statistic should be worthy of commemoration is another matter entirely.

Unless you are transfixed to the spot with amazement (or stupefied with boredom), going a few steps further down will reveal the date 1630, and the initials AM and MN. These signify the original residents of the building, Alexander Muir and Margaret Neilens. It is curious that a culture which could gleefully torch innocent women with dreadful efficiency appeared sufficiently liberated to permit a wife such public use of her maiden name after marriage.

Cannonball House will reveal one final domestic footnote to history's grand text. On the front door which opens on to the Royal Mile, there is a *petit* columnar metal contrivance known as a *risp* – the ancestor of the doorbell. Instead of emitting a dirgefully digital 'Clementine', the risp was scraped up and down the metal column to produce a din sufficiently alarming to bring the householder, and most of the neighbours, scurrying to discover which portion of the street had succumbed to an earth tremor. This must have guaranteed endless amusement and consternation at the hands of Old Town nippers playing an early version of doorabella, or worse. Did the owners of such devices leave notes on the doorstep saying 'Milkman – Please Risp'? It has a certain ring to it.

Anyway, enjoy a good rasping, thunderous risp and continue down the south side of the Mile. The next obvious landmark is the **Scotch Whisky Heritage Centre** (s3). 'Freedom an' whisky gang thegither', according to Robert Burns, though as an exciseman he ought to have known better. A visit to this imaginative social history of the barley bree will deprive you of the means for a couple of drams, but it's well worth the sacrifice, and considerably more edifying than a trip to the supermarket for cut-price Stag's Breath.

Neighbour to the whisky museum is a fine 17th century tenement, **Boswell's Court** (s4), now almost entirely devoted to the deservedly renowned Witchery Restaurant. The owner, one James Thomson, is a singular man indeed. His sombre, austere appearance, fascination for matters spiritual (he holds seances in the building's mysterious Inner Sanctum), and the decor of the restau-

rant itself have earned him the soubriquet 'The Man in Black' – an imposing title, especially for one who is known to prefer Coco-Pops for breakfast. The Witchery menu doesn't have much room for breakfast cereals: the fare is decidedly gastronomic, famous for its award-winning marriage of the best of Scottish and French haute-and-oat cuisine. Becoming a regular guest of the Man in Black is likely to send you nose-diving into the Red, but for the occasional treat there is nowhere in Edinburgh to compete. End of commercial break – nearly.

The associated enterprises of the **Cadies and Witchery Tours** (s4) likewise offer a unique and equally famous perspective on the Old Town through a winning combination of horror, humour and serious historical awareness-raising, courtesy of all the strange Men in Black one could ever hope to meet, not to mention as many of their even stranger friends. Demand for the nightly excursions is nothing less than intense, and booking is essential. Coco-Pops are *not* served during the tours.

Boswell's Court itself teems with historical associations.

Named after the uncle of the biographer James Boswell, who visited here with his subject Dr Samuel Johnson prior to departure on their famous, and infamous, Tour of the Hebrides, the building has also served as committee rooms for the Church of Scotland. By a pleasing and all too Scottish interplay of opposites, here could also be found the tryst for Edinburgh's Hellfire Club, who convened to practise the convivial art of devil-worship in the hope of conjuring up their patron to deliver an after-dinner speech.

Looming opposite the close entry is the castellated curiosity of the **Camera Obscura** (N2). This is one of several brainchilds of the brilliant Patrick Geddes (1854–1932): botanist, philosopher, and father of town-planning. As a result of his determination to see the communal identity forged over centuries in the Old Town survive as a meaningful force in the modern, fragmenting world, much of immense value in the Royal Mile has been guaranteed preservation and renewal. Geddes' vision of the city as a social space remains an invaluable corrective to the philistine bureaucracies intent on emptying the area's residents into peripheral human filing cabinets. The Camera itself is just that: a series of lenses, reflectors and twiddly bits built on a large scale to project a panoramic view of the city on to a large dais. The effect is stunning, which is good news for those who manage to survive the 90 steps it takes to reach the spectacle. Exhaustion probably contributed to the legendary remark of one wide-eyed visitor gazing at the magical vision of all Edinburgh pinholed on to the huge horizontal screen: 'How long has it been in colour?'

A little further down from the Camera Obscura is a sign denoting **Semple's Close** (N3), where lies a tiny, gem-like Old Edinburgh courtyard. Access can be gained via the adjacent close. Even during the height of summer (which usually falls on a Tuesday), this nook will be calm and cool, a square gently evocative of centuries-old Edinburgh back-courts. Two lintels bear sadly eroded but legible inscriptions:

PRAISE BE THE LORD, MY STRENGTH

AND MY REDEEMER

ANNO 1638

and

SEDES MANET OPTIMA COELO 1638

– Latin, of course, for 'Ye shoudny staun there, pal', or rather 'Your best abode is in heaven'.

Near these mottos is the image of a hand, and a curious anchor-like acronym.

The symbols indicate the arms of the Craig family, one-time inhabitants here. There is something uniquely affecting about Old Edinburgh's archive of inscribed lintels; reassuringly humble expressions of domestic security which often acknowledge, ruefully, the permanent threat of external forces. They deserve long meditation.

In complete contrast, returning to the main road and proceeding downwards brings the most memorable edifice of the Castlehill dramatically nearer. Blackened and gaunt, this Gothic revival heavenscraper (the work of James Gillespie Graham and AWN Pugin) was the Tolbooth St John's Highland Kirk and is currently **The Hub** (s5), home of the Edinburgh International Festival.

The sepulchral hue of the stone is of course not original, but stark testimony to the ravages inflicted upon sandstone by Edinburgh's smoke pollution, at one time creating a pall sufficiently thick and permanent for the affectionate pseudonym 'Auld Reekie' to arise, and stick. It might be argued that the pollution has in this case enhanced the grim visage of a Gothic masterwork. The eye is drawn magnetically ever higher up the 74 metre spire, bedecked with a gold cross which is dramatically illuminated in the evening sun. Whoever has the unenviable task of polishing the ornament must be rewarded with an Olympian view of the city: the spire, and not the Castle, marks the highest point in the Old Town.

St John's was formerly both an official church (which closed its doors in 1981), and the venue for the Church of Scotland's annual General Assembly. Old College, the dull exterior of which lies opposite on the north side of Castlehill, is now General Assembly Hall and the temporary first home of the new Scottish Parliament. To complete the ecclesiastical triangle, the Free Church of Scotland, a radical offshoot of the official Kirk formed following the traumatic Disruption of 1843, holds its Assembly in the suitably less ornate church on the corner of the Upper Bow and Johnston Terrace, just over the roundabout.

Commanding the middle ground, St John's stares down disdainfully at the schisms of Protestantism.

The religious complexities of Scotland will bring you to the end of the Castlehill; to the end of Edinburgh's and Scotland's story, never. The mini-roundabout provides a useful spot from which to photograph the St John's spire, but be quick, unless you make a hobby of close inspection of the undercarriages of taxis. Many cabbies pursue potential fares here – literally.

Jump off to the safety of the pavement, and from the Castlehill into the Mile's next instalment – the Lawnmarket – and another chapter.

CHAPTER 2

The Strange Case of the Lawnmarket

NEWCOMERS TO THE CITY or to this area of the Royal Mile might well be forgiven for concluding that 'Lawnmarket' is a striking misnomer. There is little to suggest the bustle and vigour of a colourful market thronged with eager sellers and suspicious buyers. More obviously, there's not a patch of grass in sight, even one big enough for a sparrow on a sunbed. Time can change places, even a city as relatively well-preserved as Edinburgh's Old Town. Time changes names too. The Lawnmarket used to be the *Landmarket*, where produce from the surrounding countryside was exchanged for hard cash. Lawnmarket residents today may not be short of the latter, but basic produce is another matter: they must reflect ruefully on the bustling commerce of bygone days, since the increasing commercialisation and touristification of Royal Mile retailers means that nipping out to buy bread and milk amounts to a major shopping expedition.

Perhaps it is the profusion of coffee shops, though, which has ensured the Lawnmarket's continuing prestige as the heart of the Old Town's desirable residential area. Little more than a combination of alleyways and courtyards running off the Royal Mile, the Lawnmarket's geography of twisting closes and narrow, teetering tenements is nonetheless confusing. This guide divides between the south and north sides for simplicity.

Our starting point is the **Upper Bow** (s6), a steep, cobbled street ending in a flight of steps. Although now impassable to traffic, in the days before construction of the two bridges across the Royal Mile and the hewing out of Johnston Terrace from the Castle Rock, the Upper Bow provided access into the Royal Mile from the Grassmarket and was the main route into Edinburgh from the west. From the Upper Bow, coast gently down the Royal Mile until you arrive at the opening to **Riddle's Court** (s7), one of the most attractive courtyards in the Mile.

Riddle's Court comprises two squares, the first notable for a fine wooden external stairway. No longer in use, this is one of the few surviving examples in the city of a common means of providing cheap access to upper-storey tenements. Access to the stair is possible only if you have a reason for visiting the Adult Education Centre: if you do, then you will have an excellent view of the square.

Riddle's Court holds more surprises. A sooty pend invites closer examination. Above it is the inscription VIVENDO DISCIMUS: 'we learn by living'. The portal provides access to the 'second' Riddle's Court, containing three former town-houses dating from the 1590s, built by the wealthy merchant Bailie John MacMorran. Space was at such a premium in Old Edinburgh that only the wealthiest could afford privacy, so prestigious dwellings like this one were often built according to the pattern of a courtyard; a wholly enclosed private domain adjacent to, but protected from, the teeming life of the wynds and tenements. Although now extensively restored, many fine examples of 17th century plasterwork and panelling have been preserved from MacMorran's little urban oasis and are worth seeing – assuming you can smooth-talk your way in.

Whether Bailie John MacMorran 'learnt by living' or not is difficult to ascertain, but he undoubtedly died from it. As the town bailie, he was responsible for the enforcement of law and order, and on the morning of 15 September 1595 was summoned to execute his duties in a most abnormal disturbance. Several students at the old Edinburgh High School had barricaded themselves into their hallowed hall of learning in protest against a reduction in their holidays, armed not with catapults and gobstoppers, but several guns and other assorted weapons, and sufficient provisions to sustain a long siege. This was no jolly wheeze thought up on the spur of the moment by mischievous minors, but a carefully organised manoeuvre by seasoned campaigners well-practised in 'barring out' the school authorities for similar grievances, chiefly concerning holidays. Past sieges had lasted for more than a week. One shudders to think how they expressed their displeasure with extra homework.

Failing to negotiate a settlement with the by now highly excited young rebels, Bailie MacMorran opted for a softly-softly approach and instructed his heavies to batter down the door. Panic and desperation within reached dangerous levels as the wood began to splinter, until one student, William Sinclair, opened fire from a window on the Bailie's party below. MacMorran was struck and killed. A stunned silence ensued as Sinclair's fellow-pupils capitulated without resistance, and were led away to the Tolbooth.

Sinclair and seven others stood trial, and were sentenced to death. Their privileged status as sons of wealthy and powerful families – Sinclair's father was none other than the Chancellor of Caithness – perhaps accounts for the acquittal granted to all by the 'express warrant' of James VI; harsher critics of injustice and privilege will rail at the fact that in later life Sinclair was awarded a knighthood. Incidentally, public schoolboys of today with too much homework, too few holidays and pretensions to a title are not recommended to take out a contract on the nearest magistrate.

Regaining the Royal Mile and turning right, it is easy to miss the narrow mouth of **Fisher's Close** (s8). Once within, a glance upwards evokes the towering, murky canyons of the Old Town cloisters, while ahead lies the familiarly stark juxtaposition of a prosaic contemporary world.

This inspiring monument to the vandalism wreaked upon much of Edinburgh's priceless architectural heritage during the iconoclastic wave of 1960s rebuilding – most notoriously in the expansion of the University in George Square, and the St James' Centre at the east end of Princes Street – has been known to make even the most retiring of citizens talk of plastic explosives. Rightly described by one commentator as 'an example of anti-townscape', this monstrosity at the corner of the Lawnmarket and George IV Bridge probably causes permanent damage to the retina, so perhaps it's time to go.

Parallel to Fisher's Close, yet also sadly engulfed by the same bureaucratic golgotha, is **Brodie's Close** (s9). If you get here after 5.00 pm the chances are the close will be locked. You don't need to be an historian to realise that the close is named after the father of William Brodie. Like Fisher's Close and Riddle's Court, an owner of the site is commemorated in the name. By this stage you may be far more interested in the charms of the coffee-house, certainly a far safer bet than the door opposite. This is the portal to one of the city's rolled-up trouser and exposed left-breast societies, in otherwords, the Freemasons. Once a month, the area is besieged by elderly gentlemen carrying briefcases much too small to be of practical use, except for the portage of ritual daggers and sucky sweeties for those intolerably dreary meetings. You can be sure one of these epic sessions has reached a conclusion from the sight of the aforementioned, dark-suited worthies emerging as drunk as monkeys.

Leaving the alleyway, **Deacon Brodie's Tavern** (N11) across the road cannot be missed (especially if you're a mason). The close and the pub refer not to the same person, but to father and son respectively. Brodie junior is one of Edinburgh's most celebrated rogues, though one to whom we ought to be eternally grateful as the probable inspiration for Robert Louis Stevenson's chilling fantasy of the duality of good and evil, *The Strange Case of Dr Jekyll and Mr Hyde*.

Though a terrifying nightmare was an equally powerful force behind Stevenson's brilliantly-realised tale, the story's externals could well apply to the spectacular duplicity of William Brodie. By becoming both a prosperous and respected cabinet-maker and a member of the Town Council, he followed his father's example but not in his spending habits, where he was as profligate and reckless as his father had been prudent and wise. An inveterate gambler and womaniser, he turned to burglary as a means of financing an extravagant lifestyle and servicing spectacular debts. Brodie exploited his professional knowledge ruthlessly. Not only were the more wealthy Edinburgh citizens amongst his customers, but he was also privy to precisely where their fortunes were concealed and well-placed to make copies of keys providing access to such troves.

Success as an insidious thief merely intensified Brodie's gambling habits, and the crimes became ever more daring. Protected by his cloak of respectability, one wonders what he thought – or more intriguingly, what he said – at a special meeting of the Town Council called to discuss the dramatic spate of major burglaries. His decision to take on three accomplices, and a botched attempt to rob the Excise Office on 5 March 1788, proved his undoing. He was not implicated at first, until his accomplice John Brown turned informer, and he was eventually arrested whilst attempting to escape to America from Amsterdam. George Smith – another amateur accomplice – was also arrested. Brodie and Smith were tried in Edinburgh, and sentenced to be hanged there on 1 October 1788. Before a huge crowd outside the Kirk of St Giles, Brodie the councillor and Brodie the burglar were symbolically reconciled in a final ghastly twist of fate. He was the first victim of a new 'trap-door' type of scaffold, which only a few months previously he had assisted in designing as part of his civic responsibilities. His attempts to cheat death with bribes and an iron collar proved useless. His gibbet was most efficient.

On that note of grim poetic justice we reach the end of the south side of the Lawnmarket, cross the road at the traffic lights, and proceed uphill to the top of the Lawnmarket and the entrance to **Milne's Court** (N5). Fans of *Dr Who* – or the police force – might like to note in passing that the large blue object near Brodie's Close greatly resembles the Tardis, or a Police Box, depending on your preference. If it begins to dematerialise and emit peculiar groaning noises, you've probably been overdoing it a bit. If you see a policeman emerging, you know you've completely lost your marbles, as it's been disused for years. Only daleks live in it now.

Just before you step down the passageway leading to Milne's Court, the **Ensign Ewart** (N4) tavern stretches uphill to your left. It commemorates some long-forgotten hero of the Napoleonic Wars, who is reputed to have captured, single-handedly, the standard of the French

Invincibles at the Battle of Waterloo. No doubt his pals would have been a lot happier had he stayed behind to assist in repulsing the foe instead of running off to nab a piece of coloured cloth, but nonetheless the Ensign Ewart is a fine local bar, often livened up by an excellent banjo player, who was known to regale the Duke of Wellington himself with a charming rendition of 'My Way' on the eve of famous battles.

Milne's Court is a sober and imposing affair, comprising a three-sided courtyard of eight-storey tenements. Currently a University Hall of Residence, the Court originated in an early and welcome attempt to improve the appalling living conditions of the Old Town. In 1690 Robert Mylne, master mason to the King and one of Edinburgh's first town-planners, demolished crumbling, filthy old closes to create the elegant space you see today. Or almost see, since the west quarter no longer exists, while the whole area underwent major restoration in 1971. When first built, though, the square must have appeared an architectural oasis to its fortunate first residents, providing them with access to facilities denied the average Old Towner: fresh air and a view of the sky. Hence the variety of celebrated visitors it has attracted, including Bonnie Prince Charlie, whose troops were quartered here in 1745. They arrived just a bit too early for Freshers' Week.

The eye-catching bowed iron railings on the south side are not a consequence of boisterous soldiers or students, nor evidence of carelessness at the foundry, but a pretty piece of 18th-century design. The shape of the railings permitted ladies fashionably attired in sumptuous skirts to enter the building without creasing their frocks, or injuring their modesty.

In stark contrast to the grandeur and respectability of

Milne's Court is the West Entry to **James' Court** (N6), the next opening on the left as you walk back down the Lawnmarket. Not much elegance here, but all the claustrophobic mixture of threat and intimacy of the Old Town wynds, easily appreciated by looking upwards. Have a care for the carpet-bombing tactics of the city's resident air force of dive-bombing pigeons, who continue to provide a feathered commentary of their own on Old Edinburgh's most notorious habit.

Every night at around 10 o'clock, windows would be thrown open and all the day's 'domestic waste' – more prosaically, sewage – thrown into the street below, the ritual accompanied by the splendidly euphemistic cry of *gardez loo*!, a free Scots adaptation of the French for 'watch out for the water'. Water, indeed. Those unwise enough to be passing below an open window around this time would shout nervously 'Haud yer hand!' as they scurried past. Adeptness at dodging decidedly sordid projectiles hurled from as high as twelve storeys must have been as much a matter of life and death as preservation of the original colour of one's headgear. The piles of accumulated waste would lie brewing on the street until the following morning, to be gathered into heaps by the city's 'scavengers' and sold as manure.

It is not to be wondered at, then, that Edinburgh enjoyed a reputation as one of the filthiest, foulest-smelling and most plague-ridden cities in Europe. The awesome stench of the place has elicited much wry commentary from the many emissaries from a more civilised world whose nostrils were assaulted by 'the floo'ers o' Edinburgh'. 'Most malodouriferous', commented one 16th century observer, diplomatically. More famously came the epigrammatic growl from the good Dr Johnson as he walked back to his lodgings with Boswell, shortly after slopping-out time on the night of his arrival in Auld Reekie – 'I smell you in the dark!'

Doubtless the whiff of history is becoming a little too oppressive, so refresh yourself with the cool scent of culture. Halfway down the close was the first site of the most experimental of modern Edinburgh theatres. The Traverse Theatre Club was set up in 1962 by Jim Haynes to produce innovative new theatre in an impossibly small environment. The theatre's formative years were spent in an equally atmospheric location in the Grassmarket at the bottom of Victoria Street, and the Traverse moved again in 1992 to a new and exciting space next to the Usher Hall in Lothian Road, where it continues to build upon a reputation which is now decidedly international. Intriguingly, this first site in James' Court was formerly occupied by Kelly's Paradise, specialising in performances of a rather different kind – it was an infamous Old Town brothel. (Statistics for 1740 give a total of 240 taverns and 52 brothels in the city: who carried out the research?)

Arriving in James' Court proper provides a welcome return to spaciousness and order. Due to fire, reconstruction and other ravages of time much of the original court – including half of the west side – has gone. This was the last of several Old Town addresses for David Hume before he moved to the New Town. He leased his James' Court residence to James Boswell, whose departure for larger quarters landed Hume in court over an unpaid bill. Never trust a biographer.

The north side of the courtyard today displays a series of 19th-century stained glass windows depicting ecclesiastical offices of the Church of Scotland, together with the inscription NISI DOMINUS FRUSTRA – 'It is in vain without the Lord' – motto of the City of Edinburgh. Better motto for a church, one would think.

Leaving James' Court by the mid-entry and turning left brings you to **Gladstone's Land** (N8), an entirely restored piece of Royal Mile history. Currently owned by the National Trust, this six-storey tenement is the best-preserved example of Scottish town architecture of the late

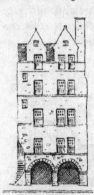

16th and 17th centuries. Access to all but the basement and ground floors is by the original turnpike stair which leads directly up from the street. This was a common feature, the ground floor originally comprising a series of open-fronted stalls leading directly on to the street, thence to customers.

Also discernible is the small nook where livestock was housed, most commonly pigs. Despite a dirty press, pigs are clean-living creatures, though their voracious appetites probably made them the welcome vacuum-cleaners of the 17th century as they hoovered up the assorted gunk jettisoned by the house-proud residents.

The most striking beast to decorate Gladstone's Land is the 'gled' – Scots for hawk – though the building's name derives not from the bird, but from the nonetheless sharp-witted merchant Thomas Gladstone, an ancestor of the more famous Prime Minister. If you can't find the hawk, then you're just not paying attention to your environment and are doubtless in need of refreshment. Nip back down the West Entrance of James' Court and you will find the **Jolly Judge** (N7), a classic Old Town 'howff' or tavern dating back to – 1980. It is a sensitive attempt to recreate the atmosphere of a small and cosy Old Town drinking den, especially alluring on cold winter nights. The games machine is a copy of a 15th-century original.

If you've made the most of the delights of the Jolly Judge, then either darkness (descended) or alcohol (imbibed), or a combination of both, will make this difficult to read. For the abstemious, instead of cutting back to the Mile, walk round the back of Gladstone's Land and you will pass another landmark, Lady Stair's House. On the south-west face of the building can be seen an unusual emblem.

This symbol testifies to another of the great perils of the Old Town – FIRE – feared almost as much as plague and famine. The clasped hands denote a 'firemark', a metal plate issued to householders by insurance companies, without which (proof of your cover) the local fire services would not so much as spit on your burning building. If the requisite insurance was beyond your financial means, then you stood and watched together with a wholly inactive team of firemen while your home was incinerated. The monstrous illogic of the system scarcely bears thinking about.

Entry to Lady Stair's House – now officially **The Writers' Museum** (N9) – is free of charge and it features exhibits devoted to the lives of three of Scotland's literary giants – Robert Burns, Sir Walter Scott, and Robert Louis Stevenson. Much of the building itself predates the lady who gave it and the close opposite its name, as the lintel above the entrance confirms. The date 1622 can be seen between the initials of William Gray and Gidian Smythe, accompanied by the customary biblical motto.

One of the house's cheekier features is a 17th century burglar-alarm. One of the interior steps is deliberately larger than the remainder, so that an intruder would be likely to trip and break his neck, rendering further defensive action unnecessary. The house once occupied the end of Lady Stair's Close, the surrounding tenements having long since disappeared to make way for **Wardrop's Court** (N10), on the west side of which you are now standing.

As you traverse Wardrop's Court to reach the east entrance next to Deacon Brodie's Tavern, you will pass Baxter's Close, though you won't realise it: another famous part of Old Edinburgh which has given up the ghost. Famous in this case because it was in a house in Baxter's Close that Robert Burns resided during his first visit to Edinburgh in 1786, when the 'heaven taught ploughman' took the fashionable coteries and literary societies of Edinburgh by storm.

The fine quartet of gryphons observing your departure from Wardrop's Court might well have something to do with Robert Burns; then again they might not, because absolutely nobody seems to know why they're there. Suggestions welcome.

As you stand at the crossroads of the Mile and George IV Bridge you are on the brink of the epic stretch of the High Street, and a correspondingly prolonged pair of chapters.

Directly ahead stands, or rather sits, a bronze statue of 18th century Edinburgh-born philosopher, David Hume, who contributed greatly to the Scottish Enlightenment. Although he blocks the pavement, he is held in high regard – in fact the locals think the sun shines out of his posterior. Seeing is believing – pop around the back of the statue and have a look.

If you cross to the south side (negotiating the synchronised green men traffic-lights is tricky, but worth it), there are three brass markers on the pavement which mark the site of the last public hanging in Edinburgh, that of George Bryce in 1864. Alternatively, crossing to the north side will reveal – particularly around 10 am Monday to Friday – a less gruesome but no less melancholy *tableaux vivant* of the dispensation of justice: groups of jurors sucking nervously on cigarettes before entering the High Court building.

It will be difficult to avoid these dark themes as we near the proud but tortured heart of the capital.

CHAPTER 3

Close to the Heart

THE HIGH STREET: the heart, the crux, the core, the nucleus, the nerve-centre, the soul, the essence, the cockpit, the distillation: all these and innumerable other metaphors, epithets and symbols have been used to denote the awfully big bit in the middle. And it is awfully big, so pay attention and follow this section very carefully – though reading while crossing the road is not recommended.

As you cross from the Lawnmarket to the High Street proper, on the left about twenty yards away is a swelling, domed, Romano-Baroque edifice, imperial in tone. It looks even more baroque at night, and arrests the attention of many visitors, puzzled by its identity: Sean Connery's Edinburgh residence? Queenie's potting-shed? Carwash for BMW owners only? Alas, none of these, though there's enough loot inside to make even a BMW blush, for this is the headquarters of the Bank of Scotland, with what the poet Norman MacCaig describes as its 'tombstone face'. By Robert Reid and Richard Crichton in 'Roman Corinthian after Palladio's manner', this monument – or mausoleum, depending on whether you are inclined towards the poetic or utilitarian view of consumption – was completed in 1806, and considerably altered by David Bryce in the late 1860s.

Opposite the High Court building and its pyre of hastily extinguished cigarettes, a squat, four-sided obelisk possesses a significance belied by its dimensions: it marks one of the few remaining wells in Edinburgh, inoperative of course since the introduction of interior plumbing. The obelisk marks the western end of **Parliament Square** (s10): for centuries the nucleus of Edinburgh's and Scotland's civic and religious life, with the Auld Kirk of St Giles' flanked by the nations' erstwhile seat of government.

Inlaid in the cobbles, near the statue of the 7th Duke of Queensberry, lies an unusual heart motif, accompanied by the figures 1430, 1386, and 1610 stamped in brass blocks. A well-known landmark for locals, this is the **Heart of Midlothian** (s11): in geographical and symbolic terms. This was the nickname of the building which once stood here, officially referred to as the Old Tolbooth Prison. Dating from 1386, the gaol was Edinburgh's first, situated next to the north-west corner of St Giles'. In reality the proximity of divine benevolence must have appeared as a cruel irony to the unfortunate inmates, for the Tolbooth provided the last stop prior to the last drop for the majority of the town's condemned criminals. Amongst thousands of less notorious and unremembered wretches, Deacon Brodie and Captain Porteous shivered away their final dreadful hours within these inexorable walls, awaiting execution in one of seven public sites in the city. The Tolbooth itself could be a place of execution, and by a cruel twist the first to ascend the scaffold here was a young boy caught robbing the house of the then Duke of Queensberry, whose descendant forever gloats upon the spectacle nearby.

Years after the demolition of the prison in 1817, the Heart was laid within an outline of the building marked by brass plates, as a memorial to the countless hearts of the condemned which doubtless hammered their last with dread and nausea. The numbers are reminders that the hangings themselves occurred at ten past four (1610), half past two (1430), and eighty-six minutes past one (1386) – or the dates of additions to the building, if you prefer.

Today the heart of stone is the source of a daily ritual which you might be fortunate enough to see for yourself. A number of local pedestrians will adroitly expectorate whilst walking past, directly into the centre of the motif, the more practised sharpshooters achieving the feat without even slowing down. Some argue that this is no more than an eloquent gesture of antipathy towards the Heart of Midlothian Football Club, while the less cynical suggest the custom is a continuation of a tradition of disrespect for capital punishment, when the spit was aimed at the impenetrable prison door. Whatever the origins of the picturesque civic mannerism, visitors were warned then – as now – not to examine the spectacle too closely on a windy day. If you want to clear your throat without embarrassment before entering the sanctity of St Giles', here's your chance.

St Giles' (S12) has been a place of worship since the year 854. In common with most ecclesiastical buildings of this scale, the finished product represents an amalgam of architectural styles embracing a lengthy period of time. The four central pillars go back to 1120, while the Albany Aisle dates from around 1409. The Thistle Chapel is a 20th-century accretion. St Giles' is best explored on a sunny afternoon, as the cool light of the north filters through the breathtaking west window. Even glorious sunbeams, however, cannot fully penetrate the oppressive and gloomy seriousness of Presbyterianism.

It will soon become obvious from the rash of plaques

and memorials adorning floor and wall that numerous Edinburgh luminaries have been commemorated here. Perhaps the two most dramatic memorials in this regard are those of the Marquis of Montrose and the Earl of Argyll. The fact that these two stare angrily at each other from opposite walls is no accident, for they remain in death as they were in life – mortal enemies. Power hungry adversaries during the Covenanting Wars and internecine bloodshed which devastated Scotland throughout most of the 17th century, Montrose's fanatical Royalism and Argyll's no less ruthless adherence to the Covenanters made them violent antagonists. When Montrose was captured in 1650, Argyll took a personal pleasure in dispatching his enemy to a thoroughly nasty execution, after which Montrose's head and limbs were impaled on spikes atop St Giles'. The grim remains of this minor poet, scholar and outstanding soldier festered on their eyrie for ten years, until the Restoration of 1660 in turn made Montrose a Scottish martyr, honoured with an elaborate and somewhat overdue burial. With a dreadful symmetry all too typical of the bloody reversals of the period, the same spikes were soon fed the corpse of Argyll, beheaded in 1661 for his part in Montrose's execution, and other 'treasonable acts'.

As well as providing a final vantage point for dismembered martyrs and traitors, St Giles' has played a prominent role in the dispensation of justice as the centre of a religion renowned for its rigid disciplinarianism. Haddo's Hole is the name given to the area above the north porch reserved for imprisoning religious enemies; not surprisingly, a busy place throughout the Covenanting period. The practice was to be short-lived, however, as parishioners soon complained of pebbles being dropped on their heads during services by the unfortunates incarcerated above.

Doubtless the worthy parishioners often vented their annoyance on the poor soul dressed in ill-fitting clothes squirming with shame from the repentance stool, situated in full view of all present. In this way the cardinal sin of fornication was made an excruciatingly public crime, punishable by hours-long, and doubtless permanently damaging, humiliation. The reintroduction of the fornicator's stool would surely provide the solution to flagging church attendance in these liberal times.

The more repressive features of Calvinist theology have of course become synonymous with the one man whose influence and teaching are indivisibly bound up with this building: John Knox. The chief architect of the Protestant Reformation of 1560 – with its revolutionary Calvinist ideal of a theocratic 'godly commonwealth' – is depicted by his statue in St Giles' as a suitably stern, steely and authoritarian prophet, though in truth Knox was an infinitely less fanatical and extreme thinker than the popular caricature of the zealous reformer, which has tended to obscure a great thinker of enormous wit and subtlety. It has even been suggested by some that this thundering orator's pulpit denunciations were delivered so *sotto voce* that St Giles' had to be sectioned off to enable the congregation to hear him.

Apocryphal or not, the legend does correspond to another characteristic of the great reformer which tends to be distorted: his humility. Knox specified a wish to be buried in an unmarked grave, and he lies in one of the city's earliest cemeteries, immediately south of his church – now a carpark for advocates. A small yellow square at parking lot 44 marks the approximate resting place of a preacher whose reflections on power-steering, private pensions and carphones would have been well worth listening to.

For a better view of Knox's godly commonwealth, or at least its capital, you could ascend the steps to the central spire of St Giles', except you're not allowed to. From this pinnacle, Sir Walter Scott had a bird's-eye view of the conflagration of 1824, which razed a substantial portion of the Old Town and damaged much more. One might have expected the impassioned Scottish antiquarian to be helping quench the inferno obliterating so many landmarks of the past, though as a self-styled member of the Scottish aristocracy, firefighting would not have featured amongst his social duties.

On the subject of blue blood, if this interests you then do not leave St Giles' without a peek at the Thistle Chapel. Located in the south-east corner, this 20th-century imitation of mock Gothic provokes mixed responses of enthusiasm for such teasing interior features as the angel playing bagpipes or the box containing the light switches under Prince Charles's seat, and revulsion for a silly piece of architectural confectionery. The chapel is the home of the Knights of the Thistle of St John, or Aristocrats in Silly Costumes, depending on your political perspective and tastes in architecture. The members of this anachronism tend to be on the whole wealthy, titled, and at least ninety years of age, making it difficult for them to lift the pseudo-medieval weaponry making up their regalia unaided. Gaudy or glorious, we now return to a more immediate world by leaving St Giles' and crossing to the south side of the Square.

Stand in front of the door to the **Signet Library** (s13) and look towards the Duke of Queensberry statue. Above the Duke's right shoulder can be seen in the distance the statue adorning the dome of the Bank of Scotland on the Mound. Look again. The wily old Duke has been sculpted in the act of throwing a frisbee – or a dustbin lid? – to his lady friend, who in turn is getting ready to execute a neat backward flip in return.

The Signet Library is part of the architectural complex housing the headquarters of the Scottish legal establishment. The library is for the sole use of advocates (the equivalent of the English barrister) researching finer points of law prior to court, or perusing angling magazines in peace. Access to the Library is only possible with permission. Through the door east of the main facade and a few steps south a colonnade leads to the Courts and Parliament Hall, the entire complex usually referred to as **Parliament House** (s14), open to the public.

Few visitors can fail to be impressed by a building redolent of Scotland's long and turbulent history which retains its grandeur as a contemporary seat of justice. Public access to the courts themselves is permitted, where the oratorical and argumentative skills of the profession can be enjoyed (quietly, in case you wake up the judge). The courts are located at the end of a passageway known as the Box Corridor, so-called because it comprises towering walls of boxes containing the reams of documents and papers no self-respecting advocate should be without. As a point of honour, no advocate disturbs or examines the papers of a colleague, so presumably a spot of rummaging and shuffling by subversive elements would bring the entire Scottish legal system to a grinding halt.

When not in court or using the library, advocates traditionally gather in Parliament Hall to discuss cases with clients and solicitors. This is the original 1639 assembly point for the Scottish parliament signed away in 1707 by the Act of Union. Today's legal business is conducted by advocates involved in earnest, perambulating conversation: walking up and down the length of the hall is the simplest way of foiling eavesdroppers. The hall certainly provides a fitting context for decorum and debate, regally decorated with an intricate stained-glass window and a hammer-beam oak roof resembling the upside-down carcass of a mighty ship. The window is the design of Wilhelm von Kaulbach and Maximilian Ainmuller – great Scottish surnames – and contains 8,000 fragments of glass. The event depicted is the 'Inauguration of the Court of Session in 1532', though 'imagined' is probably the better word: the characters' faces are fictitious, being derived from copying early photographs and transferring the images on to glass. Scotland has a distinguished record in innovation and invention, but it does not include inventing the camera in the 16th century.

Greater verisimilitude can be found in the statue of Sir Walter Scott, who as one of the Principle Clerks of Session exercised his legal duties here between 1806 and 1830 in an ambience which greatly enriched the historical substance of his fiction. If this likeness of the 'Wizard of the North' appears on the point of launching into a recital from *Waverley*, it takes second place for workmanship alongside the marble statue of Lord President Forbes. Sculpted by Louis François Roubiliac (another eminent Scotsman), this work is the oldest marble statue in Scotland, the grandiloquence and splendour of the likeness a tribute to the leniency with which the sitter treated the Jacobite rebels who were brought to book before him following the rising of 1715. Don't be fooled by his cuddly 'Well, if you *promise* not to do it again, sonny...' manner: this man was a tyrant when it came to parking fines.

The aesthetic graces adorning the building cannot dis-

44

tract for long, however, from the more unpleasant function of this space, which is a centuries-long testimony to the basest acts of humankind. All the perversions of human nature, great and small, have met their final reckoning here, most famously Burke and Hare, the so-called 'body-snatchers' who, allegedly, murdered between 16 and 30 innocent people in order to sell their corpses to doctors of medicine. Their trial during the winter of 1828 (for the murder of three people) aroused such public passion that the courtroom was daily bursting with outraged, blood-thirsty Edinburgh citizens. At one point the stench arising from the populace in whose name the villains were being tried became so overpowering that the judge ordered the opening of all the windows, despite the fact that a good-going blizzard was in progress.

If the reek of infamy, or just the whiff of the great unwashed, is becoming too pungent, step away from the rank odours of crime and look instead at the statue of a man on horseback some forty feet from the entrance to Parliament House. This dinky little number is none other than the oldest lead equestrian statue in Scotland: a fact worth memorising when you proudly show off your holi-day snaps to all those eager friends and relations too polite to ask what happened to the suntan. It is a suitably roman-ticised impression of Charles II, completed in 1685, though rumour has it that before the Restoration of 1660, it was intended to recreate the more radical majesty of Parliamentarian and scourge of monarchs, Oliver Cromwell. A combination of his sudden death, and his great unpopularity with the Edinburgh aristocracy, meant that Chuck got the nod and Olly got the boot. A close look at the face of the man on horseback might reveal a degree of compromise between Royalty and Roundhead.

The noble steed itself is no less of a curiosity. Being lead, and hollow, the old nag has suffered all the indignity of Scottish weathering over the years, most seriously when a crack in the neck admitted copious quantities of rainwater, ultimately threatening the collapse of the entire edifice. A committee of vets, engineers and architects was brought in to discover a miracle cure for the ailing beast, and elected for the brilliantly imaginative solution of drilling a small hole in the horse's undercarriage to permit the water to drain away. Where was the hole drilled? Suffice to say that this major surgery proved effective, but for ever after the memorial has been known as 'the Ghost of the Peeing Horse'.

Other quadrupeds, though less incontinent, lurk in Parliament Square: namely a collection of sphinxes. They are not at ease in the harsh Northern clime, and seem much too preoccupied with waiting for the sun to appear to pose riddles; fitting symbols, possibly, of the inscrutability and mystery of justice itself.

Return now to the Royal Mile, crossing over to the other side of the street.

Advocate's Close (N13) offers a dream-like vista of the cityscape telescoped through this well-preserved wynd. At the top end are two of the by now familiar doorway inscriptions of one Clement Cor and Helen Belenden from 1590. More interesting examples are concealed in nearby, though unfortunately inaccessible, **Byer's Close** (N12), where the former residence of Adam Bothwell, Bishop of Orkney, boasts the following (intriguingly un-Christian) inscriptions: NIHIL EST EX OMNI PARTE BEATUM (Horace), 'There is no such thing in the world as unmixed happiness'; and EXITUS ACTA PROBAT (Ovid), 'The end justifies the deed'.

Such classical worldliness is possibly more appropriate to the legal profession, and indeed both closes were favoured residences of judges and lawyers, thanks to the proximity of the courts. Weather permitting, they would lean out of their tenement windows and blether to neighbours, or discuss the relative merits of Plutarch and Pliny with colleagues, before crossing the road for another day's drudgery. In the 1750s the fourth flat in Byer's Close was home to Lord Coalstoun, a keen member of the morning window-sill committee. It is said that two young girls who lived above once lowered their cat on a string onto the revered pate of the great man. Finding a soft landing the cat dug in its claws, and was hoisted back up clinging for dear life to the judge's grandiose wig of office. Posterity does not record his worship's response to this ingenious feline comment on the fragility of human authority, but doubtless it was the talk of the close for weeks.

If you're drawn to gossip on a somewhat more global scale, then your destination should undoubtedly be the International Newsagent, stocking a plethora of international journalism from Tillicoultry to Tokyo.

A few steps down from this nexus for newsprint, the imposing presence of the **City Chambers** (N14) looms as a stark architectural contrast to the huddled Gothic of St Giles' opposite. Inside the main door – which is probably as far as you will get – is a commanding catalogue of past Lord Provosts (Scottish equivalent of the Mayor) from the year 1296. The office-holders have only presided here since the early 19th century, when the building was purchased by the Town Council. Originally completed in 1760 as the Royal Exchange, the architect John Adam provided a dignified classical work, with a pediment supported by four Corinthian pilasters, situated off the bustle of the High

Street and constructing a self-contained environment comprising a court and piazza. There were plans for expanding the space to accommodate shops, living space and a Customs House, but visions of an early city precinct came to naught. The merchants didn't like it, and preferred to continue their traditional practice of bargaining in the street: an expression of communal identity which speaks volumes for the democratic energy of Old Edinburgh's culture, and the neo-classical interpretation which would during the 18th century be imposed upon it, with variable results.

So in 1811 the merchants moved out, and the chain-gang moved in. There have been some notable holders of the office of Provost since then. There is unlucky Sir Adam Otterbourne, the only Provost of Edinburgh – and possibly in the world – to have been assassinated; and James Forrest, who had the misfortune to sleep in on the very morning he was due to welcome Queen Victoria to the city ('Sorry your Majesty, I forgot to set the alarm'). The enduring achievements of George Drummond (1687-1766) go some way towards redeeming the office of such stains – both bloody and bloody stupid – on its character. Drummond's acute political intellect, and his commitment to Edinburgh's advancement, meant that he would hold the office of provost no less than six times. He was an instigator in establishing plans for the Georgian New Town expansion north of the Old, and a founder of both the city's Royal Infirmary and Medical School. He must have had two alarm-clocks, like Sir James Millar, who had the unique distinction of being the only man ever to have been Lord Provost of Edinburgh and Lord Mayor of London – not at the same time.

It is not ex-Provosts who haunt the City Chambers,

however, but the ghosts locked into the subterranean layers of a vanished Old Town which lies in all its doric disorder beneath the cool classical facade above. The basements of the west wing of the City Chambers rest upon Mary King's Close, a thoroughfare now dark and tomb-like in a remarkable state of preservation, and with the submerged fragments of Craig's Close and Allan's Close, an unsettling timeprint capable of evoking with eerie accuracy the impossibly narrow gorges between the cliff-faces of long-ago towering tenements.

Elusiveness and mystique have helped to weave a web of fancy and superstition around this catacomb, elaborate enough to make fact and invention difficult to disentangle. Even in 1685, Mary King's Close was described in the amazingly titled *Satan's Invisible World Discovered* as a hotbed of witchery and sorcery, while to this day legends of headless dogs and other diabolic apparitions abound. Maintenance work in the last century led to the accidental discovery of the skeleton of a child immured in one of the tenement's chimneys: a fact which has frozen the blood of more than one unsuspecting visitor, and cast a permanent pall of dread over the place.

Assuming you have emerged into daylight yourself, a welcome distraction from the murk of buried history can be found in the shape of the suitably equestrian Alexander the Great in the courtyard, modelled by Sir John Steell and cast in 1883. It is an accomplished work, but Edinburgh statuary, it will now be clear, is rarely to be taken at face value. This particular nag has another rather nifty sting in its tail, or rather, ears. According to the unimpeachable authority of local rumour, Steell, upon nearing completion of his commission, found himself strapped for cash. An application for enhancement of the agreed readies fell upon deaf ears. Steell's revenge surpassed in subtlety anything he achieved as an artist. It will be observed from close examination of Alexander's cuddy's head that the mythical steed has been endowed with a pair of pig's lugs. Beware of refusing a silk purse – someone may make a sow's ear of you.

Across the road rests a narrow stone column adorned with a unicorn (ears, genuine) upon a squat, octagonal foundation. This is a Victorian reproduction of the town's **Mercat Cross** (s15), the centre of Old Edinburgh's civic culture. From here all official proclamations were delivered; monarchs pampered with wine and pageants; citizens called to arms or delivered doleful news of battles lost – all from the small balcony reached by the door in the base. In our own time, four days following the dissolution of Parliament in London – the average time taken before the petrol engine to travel between the two capitals – an analogous announcement is made from the Mercat Cross to the doubtless indifferent Edinburgh pedestrians.

Few public sites in this town are unmarked by the brutality and blood of its own and its nation's history. The Cross was the venue for many hangings, and prime location for deployment of the Maiden – the Scottish guillotine. Her steely embrace has claimed many eminent victims, the Earl of Argyll amongst them, who addressed the dreadful contrivance in his last moments in a morbid tribute as 'the sweetest maiden I have ever kissed'. He must have had some wacky girlfriends in his time.

His is not the darkest legend associated with the column. On a late summer's evening in 1513, the merchant Richard Lawson was terrified by the apparition of a 'ghostly herald' who announced in suitably sepulchral tones the imminent violent deaths of none other than King James IV, and the rump of the Scottish nobility. The list concluded with the name of Richard Lawson himself. Strangely, this did not discourage him from joining, less than a month later, the King's 10,000 strong army on its march south to engage the English in a wholly unnecessary battle under the terms of the Auld Alliance between Scotland and France. The bloodbath of Flodden Field on 9 September, in which the King was hacked to pieces along with the cream of the Scottish aristocracy and most of his army, delivered a devastating blow to the rich Renaissance flowering of the country and bit deeply into Scottish consciousness. Lawson was to survive and pass his story down, in what must rank as the most extreme example in history of the consequences of not sharing a secret. Alternatively, perhaps his fantastic tale was elaborated in retrospect to dramatise how truly miraculous was his escape from the most appalling massacre of Scotland's military history.

A little down from the Cross's present location (it has been shifted numerous times to make way for the vicissitudes of progress), **Old Fishmarket Close** (s16) drops steeply down from the main road. The tantalising aromas emanating from the excellent brasserie Le Sept have thankfully superseded the erstwhile whiff of the thoroughfare, once affectionately described as 'a stinking ravine' because of the early 19th-century fishmarket. The cuisine on offer then was decidedly a la cart: ranks of wooden trestles slippery with scales and brine from the piles of unwashed and uncured harvest from the sea. One of the fishwives working here, Maggie Dickson, is a figure of Edinburgh legend, though not because of her dexterity with the filleting knife. On 2 September 1724, she miraculously revived a few hours after her public hanging. Her resurrection from the coffin on the back of the cart conveying her to her final resting-place gave the driver a near-fatal shock, and the city magistrates a legal and moral headache. Should she be re-hung? How do you execute a person whose death certificate has been signed? After the first week of intensive debate the committee specially convened to resolve the case were still in deadlock as to whether 'hanged' or 'hung' was the correct term to use. Councillor Snoddy led the *hanged* faction, councillor Shanks the *hung*; while councillor Priddle is on record as saying he didn't give a s*** about all this pratting about with semantics, as far as he was concerned the only f****** hanging he could see was f****** hanging around, and unless this useless bunch of s**** got their fingers out of their a****, the woman would have died of natural causes anyway. This was inspirational. The crisis was resolved by opting for the intervention of divine providence: the committee was delivered, and so was Maggie Dickson. She lived for a further thirty years and raised a family. The nasty scar she bore until the (natural) end of her life may have been less of a potent reminder of her deliverance than the nickname – half-cruel, half-kind – by which the Old Town soon knew her: 'Half-Hangit Maggie'.

In a peculiarly Edinburgh-like coincidence, Maggie Dickson's less than thorough executioner lived next to her place of work. At the base of the close on the right, on the site now occupied by the new sheriff court, appropriately enough, stood a lowly dwelling reserved as official residence for Edinburgh's hangman. As the incumbent was the target of continual verbal abuse and of projectiles in varying stages of putrefaction, it is difficult to know whether the free house constituted a substantial perk, or an essential means of personal protection. Likewise, the specially reserved seat in St Giles' for the council's legalised murderer was doubtless a privilege of a similarly academic nature, since nobody in their right mind would sit anywhere near him.

Not surprisingly, the post has attracted some charismatic and sensitive individuals. Alexander Cockburn (1681-82) relished his work so much that he found some overtime out of office hours and strangled a 'bluegown' or privileged beggar: for his professional dedication, a colleague and rival from Stirling, Mackenzie, came down to Edinburgh to execute the executioner. John Scott, Edinburgh's last official hangman, is remembered for similar reasons. On 12 August 1847, he entered the record books by becoming the only public executioner to be murdered while still in office. His assailant, John Eddie, is unironically described in the city records as 'an alcoholic watchmaker'. His execution, sadly, has deprived the world for good of the timepiece which informs the wearer 'who caresh about the time, lesh have shomething to drink' – and goes hic hoc, hic hoc.

Yesh, time to go. Continue down the Mile past the Fringe Office, the function of which will be self-explanatory – especially if you're reading this in August, in which case it will take you the rest of the day to negotiate the ticket queues and hordes of handout-touting luvvies, selling everything from Shakespeare to Stand-up in the most extraordinary theatrical festival in the world.

Escape the hordes by crossing over to **Anchor Close** (N15), which has no nautical associations whatsoever, taking its name from a famous tavern once situated here.

Before its large-scale demolition and reconstruction in 1868, Anchor's Close was home to Downey Douglas', another of Old Edinburgh's epic bevvy of howffs hosting a plethora of drinking clubs and societies. The Crochallan Fencibles met here, numbering among them men of learning and letters like Robert Burns and the club's founder, William Smellie, one of the luminaries of Edinburgh's once mighty publishing industry, and father of the *Encyclopedia Britannica*. Offering serious drinking and serious intellectual debate in equal measure, these learned societies proved fertile ground for the spectacular flowering of Edinburgh into 'a hotbed of genius' in the latter half of the 18th century, when the brilliant achievements of the Scottish Enlightenment turned Edinburgh into the 'Athens of the North', and an intellectual capital of Europe.

Assuming you wish to preserve your own portable capital for the sake of further intellectual exploration of your own, there is a wide range of emporiums, restaurants and hostelries of variable quality you will need to pass before reaching the next road on the right, Hunter Square.

On the far side is the **Tron Kirk** (s17), now a disembowelled and excavated carcass serving as a part-time exhibition and information centre for the Old Town, and very useful it is too. The denuded interior is dramatic, notably the intricacy and grandeur of the timber roofing, while beneath it a fascinating archaeological excavation under the floor has exposed a network of former closes and wynds. Here another page in the history of the Old Town has been uncovered, the 16th-century Marlin's Wynd, named after the Frenchman credited with first cobbling the High Street.

The Tron Kirk itself dates from 1648, though the spire is a restored version of the one destroyed in the fire of

1824. 'Tron' refers to the old weighing-machine once attached to the exterior, where merchants' goods were weighed to determine their value prior to sale. Unscrupulous traders paid dearly for any devious practices. They would be bound with rope to the central beam, and then secured more intimately by means of a nail hammered through the ear into a post. In humiliation and agony the miscreant would be thus left part-crucified all day. A combination of this and the torments of the public proved so unendurable for some victims that they would tear the ear off in their desperation to escape. That this drastic recourse was deemed 'permissible' under the law –presumably because escape caused even greater pain – only compounds the barbarism of the legislation.

Rubbing your ear uncomfortably, the end of the first section of the High Street is in sight, marked by the intersection of the North and South Bridges – twin viaducts and remarkable feats of engineering. The current **North Bridge** (N16) dates from 1897, and is its third incarnation. The first attempt to link the Old and New Towns – a distance of less than half a mile, but separating two worlds – partially collapsed in 1769, killing five people (perhaps the only disaster in which the worthy George Drummond was implicated: he laid the foundation stone). Upon re-opening three years later a further problem became apparent: the dangers of Edinburgh's excessively violent winds, necessitating the addition of balustrades to prevent luckless pedestrians from losing hats, or being blown off themselves.

A slightly more modest and less windswept affair, the **South Bridge** (S18) is a nice example of the art which conceals architecture. It consists of 19 arches, of which only one – spanning the Cowgate – is visible. The first vehicle to use the bridge when it opened in 1789 was a hearse, containing an old worthy who had expressed a final wish to be the first to traverse the new structure. Little competition was probably faced. According to a long-held Scottish superstition, the first living thing to cross a new bridge is eternally damned. The belief was still sufficiently potent in the late 19th century for a herd of sheep to be made the first creatures to reach the other side of the new Forth Railway Bridge, completing the crossing in a time which no train has yet managed to beat. It is said that somewhere in the fabric of the Forth Road Bridge, completed in 1963, there is a mouse superstitiously buried; presumably a farmer suitably generous couldn't be found to provide a sheep for the purpose. There was, in fact, a person damned by the Forth Road Bridge just after it opened: the man in the wee booth who stopped the first car and asked the driver for toll money. Incidentally, the Forth Railway Bridge contains over seven million rivets, and during its construction a special boat was commissioned to row around the structure and retrieve the hundreds of caps belonging to the labourers which had been blown into the water while they worked in the fierce winds.

If you are having difficulty in finding some way of establishing connections between the content of the last two paragraphs and the continuation of Edinburgh's High Street, this is hardly surprising. So put your nice woolly little lamb back on its lead, and trot off across the junction of the South Bridge and the High Street, being careful not to step on the rodents' gravestones.

CHAPTER 4

To the World's End

HERE LIES ONE OF the most contentious architectural projects of recent times in the city, the Crowne Plaza Hotel. A luxury establishment on a massive scale with some 240 rooms, this hybrid dream of mock baronial and mock vernacular by Ian Begg has provoked both gasps of awe and streams of expletives since its completion in 1990. Those in favour welcome the filling of a hideous Royal Mile gapsite with sensitive reconstruction, those against deplore the Disneyfication of the Royal Mile into a tartan theme-park. Whatever one's view of the impact of the work, the interior remains a visionary variation on the international style – that is to say, with all the aesthetic merit of an airport departure lounge. The totality of the building has swallowed up the sites of three former closes, and one former brothel, though it might be advisable not to enquire about the location of the latter should the visitor wish to partake of the hotel's truly excellent range of services.

The entrance to **Carrubber's Close** (N17) beckons as a blast of authenticity from the opposite side of the road in contrast to all this plush pastiche. This is where Allan Ramsay, the former wigmaker and bookseller who turned to poetry and became a seminal figure in the 18th century vernacular literary revival, opened Edinburgh's first playhouse, the New Theatre, in 1736. The gifted anthologiser of the Scottish poetic tradition who produced the definitive *Evergreen* and *Tea-Table Miscellany* intended to invest his literary success by performing a similar service for Scotland's theatrical life, badly in need of a kick up the proscenium. But barely one year later the venue was closed down when the government proscribed theatrical performances outside of London. Ramsay's infuriated complaint that such blatant centralist interference effectively reduced Scotland's capital to the status of a provincial 'clachan' has a depressing relevance to cultural politics in the present.

The ghost theatre eventually became a venue for an assortment of Edinburgh's burgeoning intellectual societies. By 1858, with the dazzling diamond of the Edinburgh Enlightenment a nostalgic glint, it was home to a charming atheistic sect known as the 'Celebrated Cathedral of the Prince of Darkness', which was hastily extinguished by respectable Victorian Edinburgh. The building was repossessed, doubtless exorcised of pernicious cultural and satanic influences, and consecrated as the Whitfield Chapel. The last laugh must go to Auld Nick himself, though, for the chapel was flattened in 1872 as a part of an urban redevelopment scheme.

In a small courtyard at the back of **Bailie Fyfe's Close** (N18), careful inspection will reveal a crumbling lintel with this melancholy couplet:

ENEMIES OF GOD AND THE KING

TO THE EARTH DID ME DOWN DING

1572

Edinburgh was undergoing one of the worst periods in its history at the time this haunting cry was chiselled into permanence. Civil war raged between the 'King's Men' and the 'Queen's Men': supporters of the infant King James VI, and his mother Mary Queen of Scots, respectively. A bloody struggle between Court and Kirk, Catholic and Protestant, for the very soul of the country itself was raging, and the city occupied centre stage. Only English invasion brought eventual settlement and a period of relative tranquility to the capital, under the far from satisfactory regency of the Earl of Morton. His charge, the twelve-year-old James VI, retrieved his authority in 1578. It is difficult to unravel the precise meaning of the inscription's condensed allusions, but as a poignant and laconic reflection on dire times it 'dings' with the awful certainty of a death-knell.

The courtyard can be left by another alley – **Paisley Close** (N19) – remembered for the 'Heave Awa' disaster of November 1861. In the middle of the night, a large section of an old tenement collapsed, killing thirty-five of the innocently slumbering residents. While the rubble was being cleared in the grim aftermath of the search for corpses, workers heard the faint but determined shouts of encouragement from a boy buried alive under piles of masonry and timber: 'Heave awa', chaps, I'm no deid yet!' The blunt and sanguine humour of his request has been immortalised in stone immediately above the close's entrance, though in a somewhat anglicized form, in accordance with Victorian notions of Scottish dialect and, doubtless, politeness. What the poor lad with the tenement on his head *really* said is probably unrepeatable, though you can bet your life it wasn't chaps.

The **Museum of Childhood** (S19), across the main road,

must rank as the only museum in the world where gleeful noise is positively encouraged, and a visit is strongly rec-

ommended – not least because entrance is free. Whether or not contemporary youngsters have succumbed too far to the introverted, imagination-stifling banalities of mega-death computer culture to respond to this captivating storehouse of Victorian and Edwardian playthings, it is difficult to say. Most children from the age of 25 upwards, though, should experience the delights of rediscovering the Peter Pan alive in every adult, and this is precisely the place in which to let him loose for a while.

Over the street is Carrubber's Christian Centre. An evangelical establishment from the mid-19th century, its architecture has certainly won few converts: the edifice was described in the Builder magazine as 'a miserable production, exhibiting in a feeble farcical manner the most commonplace details of the style of Palladio'. One gets the feeling they didn't like it.

At one time the nearby **Moubray House** (N20) was the base for production of the *Edinburgh Courant*, an early local newspaper, whose editor in 1710 was Daniel Defoe. This was surely a strange cover for one sent to Edinburgh as a spy for the English Government prior to the corruption-ridden Act of Union of 1707, his brief to prevent anti-Union activities and, splendidly, to 'remove the uneasiness of the people about secret designs here'. You can trust me completely, I'm a government spy. Ah, British democracy.

More might be learnt about Moubray House were the

heritage market not monopolised at this corner by the adjacent 15th century **John Knox House** (N21), the most seriously misnamed dwelling in the whole of Edinburgh, since the preacher almost certainly never lived here. The statue on the south-west corner of the building is not, as many assume, a likeness of Knox but of the prophet Moses, though it would be pardonable to confuse the two. The little figure on the sundial is depicted pointing to a representation of the sun (the inscription reads 'imagine having to go and get commandments on a day like this'), and for a time was encircled by a miniature pulpit. It would seem the aim was to co-represent Knox in mid-sermon with his distinguished Biblical colleague, in a gesture of reciprocal honour to both, but the end result has been to exasperate guides who must constantly reiterate their polite explanation to the effect that John Knox never lived here, and Moses never got quite as far as Edinburgh either, in spite of parting the waters of the Firth of Forth and finding somewhere to buy bread on a Sunday.

If scholarly research one day established beyond doubt that Knox never actually knocked on this door, it would probably alter the building's identity and its appeal to visitors not one whit, such is the power of the tourist industry to exploit, at its best, historical speculation and doubt; at its worst, make-believe and myth.

Unless a collection of bibles is your particular pot of mince, forego What's-his-name's House and instead duck down **Tweeddale Court** (S20). In 1806 there was a particularly nasty robbery and murder on this spot, the victim a bank porter named William Begbie. The assassins scarpered with £4,392, a hefty percentage of the entire stock of the British Linen Bank, the headquarters of which the unfortunate employee was trying to reach. Prior to its financial days the building was a wealthy town house, and a careful eye will manage to identify the sole surviving example of a shelter in which the sedan chairs – the preferred method for traversing the Old Town for those too dignified to be seen walking – were stored. The carriers must have taken a deep breath or two before lugging portly noblemen up to the Lawnmarket.

Prepare for the end of the world, which is imminent: both a close and a pub confirm that beyond this block lies the void. Well, the Canongate, to be precise, but for Old Edinburgh a vitally important boundary, defended by the magnificent Netherbow Port, the immense gateway to the city which so often provided salvation, and just as often admitted disaster. For the many citizens whose parameters were defined by the city walls, this point marked, quite literally, the end of the world: beyond lay the horrors of Leith, wolves, and England.

World's End Close (S21) was formally known as Sir James Stanfield's Close, after a prosperous English manufacturer who resided in the area and probably owned much of the property too. Rich certainly, but evidently not popular. One morning in November 1687, Stanfield's drowned body was dragged from a nearby pool. Suicide was the supposed cause, but on account of the ostentatious manner in which his family conducted the burial, and the somewhat incriminating detail that Stanfield's widow had purchased her mourning clothes several days prior to her husband's unfortunate demise, murder was soon cried. Eventually two surgeons exhumed and examined the corpse, and established strangulation as the cause of death.

In accordance with contemporary legal practice, the investigators proceeded to torture the Stanfield family servants, who proved eager to reveal a family plot in which the son Phillip emerged as the likely instigator and assailant. Despite the conclusive forensic evidence of the surgeons, science deferred to superstition in the form of the grim practice known as 'the ordeal of touch'. A suspected murderer was made to touch the corpse of the putative victim, and guilt was established beyond doubt, on the authority of divine revelation, if the cadaver began – miraculously, or at least unaccountably – to bleed. Modern science can suggest several more rational and secular explanations for the phenomenon, but Phillip Stanfield was born a few centuries too soon, and passed the test with flying colours. James Millar depicted the grisly proceedings thus:

> *Young Stanfield touched his father's corpse*
> *Where rose a fearful wail*
> *For blood gushed out the winding sheet*
> *And every face grew pale.*

This last recorded instance of the grotesque ritual in Scotland 'pales' in comparison with the execution to which it inevitably led. On 15 February 1688 Phillip Stanfield was hanged. His tongue was cut out. His hand was cut off. His head was likewise severed, then dispatched to Haddington for public display. What little of his mortal remains that were left were hung in chairs regularly positioned between Edinburgh and Leith. The evil of the young man's crime is beyond dispute, but was it any worse than the horror of this cynically protracted public butchery?

For the answer to such sophisticated moral dilemmas, where better to turn than an arts centre and theatre? The **Netherbow Arts Centre (N22)** lies opposite, the small-scale venue with large vision which specialises in contemporary theatre. Inside this miniature citadel for creativity can be seen a sonorous bell which once adorned the original Netherbow Port. The Port has long since vanished, but the ancient gateway to Leith, wolves and England reveals another and slightly more eccentric memorial on the wall above tenement no. 9, bearing the paradoxical information ERECTED 1873: DEMOLISHED 1764. The earlier date refers to the dismantling of the Port, while the later indicates the unveiling of the plaque. Nice of them to explain it, but then the march of history is often said to run in the wrong direction in Scotland.

Once occupying the entire width of the large road junction before you, the precise location of the Port is indicated on the road surface. Looking south down St Mary's Street, in the distance an original section of the Old Town wall to which the Port was joined is unmistakable. Step from the safety of this chapter and the old defences and head east. In historical terms you are no longer in Edinburgh. Don't throw the book away, though – just turn the page into the last stage of your journey.

CHAPTER 5

A Holy Happy Land?

ETYMOLOGISTS REJOICE! The final instalment of the Royal Mile is, like the Lawnmarket, deceptive in terms of nomenclature. *Canongate* refers not to an elaborately armoured portal, but to the decidedly more passive values of the Augustinian monks formerly based at the Abbey of Holyrood. The street you are now entering was the *gait* – Scots for walk or road – which evolved between their cloisters and the city.

Not until the construction of the Palace of Holyroodhouse in the 16th century did the Canongate develop into a distinctive settlement, colonised by noblemen, officials, retainers, cooks, bottle-washers and assorted hangers-on to the Court. The area subsequently grew in size and status to become a burgh autonomous from Edinburgh, with its own council, magistrates and prison, preserving its independence until it was swallowed up by the capital in 1856. Even today, more elderly Canongatians can be heard to state that they do not consider themselves to be residents of Edinburgh, to the puzzlement of passers-by. There is an unmistakably individual atmosphere here though, and the higher proportion of residential property than in the remainder of the Mile heightens the contrast.

The Canongate commences with an eclectic array of shops – everything from sticky buns to oriental rugs. On the north side **Cranston Street** (N23) peels off to the left, the avenue notable only perhaps for its former reputation. This iniquitous little thoroughfare once boasted two of the city's 240 brothels, located in large tenements nicknamed

Happy Land and Holy Land. Whilst the establishments have long since disappeared, the irreverent irony with which the natives of Edinburgh christened them is as strong as ever.

More immediate incongruity is evident further down the north side, in the form of a small statue above and to the right of the entrance to Mid Common Close. Reputedly a Moorish figure, the sculpture has helped to formalise the appellation **Morocco Land** (N24) for the tenement. Why a Moor should be found commemorating a grey, wind-blasted Scottish tenement as unremarkable as this one – unless he got lost en route for Happy Land in search of his harem – has encouraged the spinning of more yarns than a cotton-mill, ranging from the exotic and the fantastic to the plain daft.

Making sense of this accumulated fabricated folklore would keep a library full of postgraduates busy for years. Most of the tales connect the bust in some way with a local lad, Andrew Gray. Allegedly, during the celebrations for the coronation of Charles 1 in 1633, Gray and an assortment of ne'er-do-wells hijacked the festivities, and demonstrated their distaste for the city's Lord Provost, Sir John Smith – who was also Gray's uncle – by burning his effigy. In the ensuing and time-honoured Edinburgh riot, the ringleaders were arrested, and Gray was sentenced to be hanged. With Gray's cronies mounting a daring raid of the Tolbooth in which the condemned man slipped the noose and fled overseas, plausibility and pretence remain on nodding terms – just.

The best is to come. It emerges that during his twelve-year exile, Gray fell in with a Moroccan Emperor/Pirate Ship/Interplanetary Spacecraft (tick in order of preference), returning to Edinburgh in 1645 as the captain of a

Moorish vessel. In that year the city was in the grip of its last, but also its worst, dance of death with the bubonic plague. When the Moroccan crew supposedly held the city to ransom, there were no soldiers left to defend it, forcing the Lord Provost to negotiate with the Turbaned Gray. Cue heroine. By an extraordinary coincidence, the Lord Provost's Beautiful Daughter was a bit peely-wally with the plague, melting the heart of good old TG, who vowed to renounce all thought of revenge and cure the BD with the aid of some conveniently acquired Magical Powers. Undoubtedly good old TG had a fair command of the MP, succeeding in doing what medical science would fail to do for a further two hundred years, restoring BD to her Overjoyed Father. In gratitude and in honour of TG's MPs, TG was thereafter granted full forgiveness for past sins by OF and declared a civic hero. And oh, yes, just one last small detail. TG and BD fell madly in love and lived happily ever after in the tenement they built and called Morocco's Land.

Well, yes, TSIALOB (This Story Is A Load Of Bull). If you seek slightly less imaginative explanations, the figurine may reflect expansive trade relations with Africa: then again, it could well be Mrs Hetty McSnoddy's prize-winning piece in the annual exhibition of the Canongate Community Arts Class for 1963.

Chessel's Court (s22) opposite and further down the Royal Mile, on the other hand, takes its name from the Arabian princess, born in Edinburgh, who introduced a famous board game with 24 pieces to the Western world, and you can believe that if you want to. Extensively reno-vated last century, the principal building on the south side of the quadrangle dates from 1745. This was the Excise Office, the target for Deacon Brodie's spectacularly botched heist on 5 March 1788, which helps to account for the fear of the citizens in the area to this day, indicated by the Neighbourhood Watch sign. On the other hand, it has been suggested that the warning has nothing to do with crime, but indicates the popular local pastime of observing the remarkable behaviour of residents emerging from an evening in the adjacent Mexican restaurant, displaying the spectacular side-effects of raw chillies and a pint of mescal.

A little further on is **Old Playhouse Close** (s23). The theatre enjoyed a long life by Edinburgh standards – 1747 until 1769 – but its popularity might have had more to do with the frequent fisticuffs and brawls, which were a familiar accompaniment to a good night out, than the aesthetic merit of the productions. A famous set-to ensued in 1749 on the anniversary of the Battle of Culloden, when English officers in the audience commanded the orchestra to strike up the inflammatory air 'Culloden'. In spirited defiance, the musicians cheerfully responded with the opening chords of the Jacobite 'You're Welcome, Charlie Stuart', at which point a virtual re-enactment of the battle itself took place, with chairs and swords figuring prominently. The scene is re-enacted annually at the Tron Church on New Year's Eve at the stroke of midnight, where the chairs and swords are replaced by empty whisky bottles sported by various inebriates intent on giving a French kiss to everyone in sight.

On the surface of the road outside Old Playhouse Close, a large cross denotes both the old boundary of the Canongate, and the nearby former residence of the Knights of St John: **St John's Street** (s24) can be found some 15 yards further on. Several of these knights attended the Canongate Kilwinning Masonic Lodge here. Dating from 1736, the hall is believed to be the oldest surviving lodge in the world, with the added claim to fame that Robert Burns became affiliated to the chapter on 1 February 1787. A hitherto unknown verse or two on the intricacies of the rolled-up troosers by the National Bard would be literary gold-dust.

Opposite lies a large tenement (numbers 197–171) displaying two complementary emblems, of which the specimen above the first-floor window of number 185 is decidedly the more dramatic. This tablet displays a Psalter open at Psalm No. 133, reproducing the first verse. What a relief to find the refreshingly literal derivation of **Bible Land** (N25) for the tenement – almost. It was the manufacture of (non) holy footwear rather than scripture which took place here. Above the Psalter, a crown and rounding-knife are visible: icons associated with King St Crispin, Patron Saint of the cobblers who plied their trade in this area.

During extensive restoration of the building in the 1950s, several manuscripts penned by one Alexander Profeit at the beginning of the century were discovered concealed behind a wall. Work must have ground to a standstill after the first few lines of the secret journal were perused, since they comprised a searing indictment of the corrupt and dissolute lifestyles of various Canongate residents. The tirade was reburied but not before the document was transcribed. Maybe it's just a load of old Crispins concocted by a sad old man.

On the south side lies **Moray House** (S25). Scotland's principal teacher-training college adjoins St John's Street, and originated in 1625 as a conspicuous property amongst the townhouse set who brought to the Canongate its exclusive, court-blessed residential uniqueness. Both Charles 1 and Oliver Cromwell are said to have been guests here, though probably on alternate nights. Some historians think the house might have been the venue where Cromwell and the Earl of Argyll deliberated the execution of the King. Two years later, on 18 May 1650, the celebrations of a wedding party of Argyll's at Moray House were interrupted to permit guests to move to the balcony and spit and hurl abuse at a figure passing below. This was the Marquis of Montrose, bound to a high chair and being led up to Parliament House to receive his death sentence. It must have been a tight squeeze for the gloating guests: firstly, there's no door on to the balcony; secondly, it's hardly accommodating. Another instance of unreliable folklore, or interesting historical evidence of the Earl of Argyll's tight-fisted hospitality.

The **Canongate Tolbooth** (N26) further down on the north side should not be missed, in both senses. Much of the fussiness of the building, including the delicate flourish of the mammoth clock, are silly Victorian accretions from the 1880s. The Tolbooth is of 16th century design, and an ostentatious expression of a burgh's pride. Franco-Scottish in style, the tower features conical roofed bartizans with quatrefoil gunloops, with further splayed gunloops punctuating a formidable appearance. The detailed defences are in fact almost purely decorative. Ironically, behind the bluster the building was no great shakes as a fortification, and positively leaked inmates. With the opening of a new city gaol on Calton Hill in 1848, as difficult to penetrate as to escape, the Tolbooth let its prisoners out for the last time.

At other times the Tolbooth has served – probably slightly more successfully – as a fire-station and a venue for council meetings with little worth leaking. It is now devoted exclusively to a museum, **The People's Story** (N26). Before entering, connoisseurs of the Latin motto – if there are any left by now – might try, next to the Canongate emblem, SIC ITUR AD ASTRA, commonly translated as 'this way to the car park', though its true meaning is 'pathway to the stars'. More inscriptions on the facade profess loyalty to the monarch and animadvert on the virtues requisite to a prince. Only the canny observer will notice, by the east corner of the tower, a selection of seashells embedded in the stonework: an intricate decorative gesture for warding off evil spirits and double-glazing salesmen.

The comprehensive displays of the museum revel in much spiritedness, of the public variety: entrance is free to this imaginative recreation of the conditions of the average citizen from the late 18th century to the present. Documents, photographs, videos and a panoply of material culture, authenticated by oral reminiscence, combine to make a sensitive annal of social history. More fascinating information can be gleaned from the amenable guides, who are fond of a blether which enlivens the static displays.

Across the road lies the sister museum of **Huntly House** (S27), equally worth a long visit. A quartet of 16th century Latin inscriptions, together with a restoration plaque, have earned the building its popular name of 'the Talking House'. From east to west, the inscriptions read:

ANTI QUA TAMEN JUVEN ESCO (1932)

– I am old, but renew my youth

HODIE NISI CRAS TIBI CUR IGITUR CURAS (1570)

– Today for me, tomorrow for thee, why therefore carest thou?

UT TU LINGUAE TUAE, SIC EGO MEAR(UM) AURIU(M) DOMINUS SUM

– As thou art master of thy tongue, so am I master of my ears

CONSTANTI PECTORI RES MORTALIUM UMBRA

– Moral affairs are a shadow to a steadfast heart

SPES ALTERU VITAE

– There is another hope of life

If the crick in the reader's neck permits, there is a feast of artefacts from Edinburgh's history awaiting inside: a section of the original Covenant of 1638; shop-sign of the snuff manufacturer James Gillespie; a model reproducing the High Street and Netherbow Port as they were in the 16th century; Greyfriars Bobby's collar; Cadies' badges; James Craig's plans for the New Town, to name but a fraction. The porcelain and glassware may inspire less, but the truth of a people's history emanates as strongly from its trivia. As companion museums, the Tolbooth and Huntly House comprise a cultural record of immense value.

The wonderful courtyard within **Bakehouse Close** (s26) is easy to miss, but difficult to forget. Its blackened pend testifies to a once filthy city: within, the now mute buildings are redolent of the noisy energy which once filled them. Records reveal that living conditions in this nook were as appalling for the poor as they were in the High Street. The census return for 1851 records that 230 people were crammed into this space, and the **Canongate Kirkyard** (N27) on the opposite side of the road is an appropriate reminder of the shockingly high mortality rate, though few of the poor could afford a gravestone.

Distinctly different from other Edinburgh kirks, the Dutch Reform style of the **Canongate Kirk** (N27) provides a welcome contrast to more austere places of worship. The south facade is emblazoned with the Royal crest of King James VII, presiding over a more subdued memorial to

Thomas Moodie, who funded the establishment of the kirk. Beneath the plaque a tablet boldly proclaims that the building was constructed according to the express wish of the King; neglecting to add that only because the monarch evicted the Canongate congregation from Holyrood Abbey was the kirk necessary in the first place.

The silent majority are brought to mind, too, by the modest metal container cemented to a stone pillar on the south side, to the left of the entrance. This is an original poorbox. With these dimensions to charity, no wonder the poor were poor.

The kirk is usually open for inspection, though the histories in stone to be found in the graveyard are possibly of greater interest. Adam Smith, author of *The Wealth of Nations* (1776) and the father of modern economics, rests in the south-west corner. The fact that coach-loads of Japanese tourists make this their first point of pilgrimage after Edinburgh airport might have amused this doyen of Edinburgh's intellectual Golden Age, though he is more likely to turn in his grave. Smith's sensitive anatomy of capitalism has become an ideological cloak for the ruthless monetarism shamefully promoted in his name by right-wing governments today, who monopolise the principle of the 'free market' in ways which would have appalled him.

Some 80 feet due north from the sober Smith sits a memorial to the reckless Robert Fergusson, another genius of 18th century Scottish letters, though not so much misremembered as not remembered enough. Only twenty-four years of age when he died, alcoholic and insane, in

Edinburgh's Bedlam, Fergusson's fitful poetic career established him as Scotland's greatest satirical observer of 18th century streetlife. The wit and

energy of his depictions of the capital inspired many, most notably a young Robert Burns, who confessed that without Fergusson's example he would never have become a poet. Fittingly, it was Burns himself who commissioned this headstone in memory of a poet buried thirteen years earlier in an unmarked grave. Burns dedicated it to 'my elder brother in misfortune, by far my elder brother in the muse'.

The persistent stereotype of Burns as philanderer who penned a couple of gems in his spare time can be found alive and well by crossing to the east wall of the graveyard, where a bronze relief in line with the centre of the kirk commemorates one Nancy M'Lehose. This was the 'Clarinda' with whom Burns, as 'Sylvander', started a passionate and spiritual affair, mainly through letters, during the winter of 1787. Reading Burns' work is time much better spent than pursuing all this prurient nonsense, though for those who like that sort of thing, that is the sort of thing they like.

Also on the east side, an ancient and weathered stone casket is reputed to contain the remains of David Rizzio, unfortunate multi-punctured Royal favourite, of whom more presently. Keen gravehunters can seek out several more celebrities, like the worthy Lord Provost George Drummond, for example, though one is advised to confine such research to daylight hours. Under cover of darkness, the restless souls of the dead will prove positively reassuring in comparison to regular visitants from the present, intent on experiencing spirits of quite a different kind.

On the way out, two further sculptures are worth a nod. The first, the Canongate version of the Mercat Cross, stands in the south-east corner of the kirkyard, enjoying dignified retirement from several ages spent in the middle of the Canongate thoroughfare. In contrast, the fountain memorial to the Victorian psychic Daniel Douglas Hume (1833–1886) has not so much been moved as 'caused to disappear'. The monument to this seer (whose services Queen Victoria herself enlisted) used to lie just inside the kirkyard, but it vanished in 1951, its ruinous condition judged by the city authorities to represent a health hazard. In 1959, at the end of an eight-year quest, a member acting on behalf of the *Psychic News* traced what little remained of the fountain and purchased, for an unspecified sum, the stump of its plinth. This fragment is now in the possession of the Edinburgh College of Parapsychology.

A little further on, and a well-kept secret, is **Dunbar's Close** (N28). The former wasteland to the rear was transformed in 1980 into a replica 17th century town garden, under the auspices of the Mushroom Trust – an anonymous body, and with a name like that, little wonder. The garden comprises a series of ornamental trees, hedges and lawns, and despite its geometrical order represents a refreshingly natural oasis from the midsummer madness with which the Mile nearby is afflicted. This jewel, be reassured, offers public privacy – but please don't tell anybody. The company director of Witchery Tours likes to play with his collection of used envelopes here on days off. The Victorian letterbox outside the nearby post office guarantees delivery within a generation or two.

Crichton's Close (s28) is home to **The Scottish Poetry Library,** which apart from containing a definitive archive of Scottish and international verse also functions as an important cultural resource centre to encourage debate, dialogue, and revision of the absurd stereotypes which surround this most vital of art forms. And as the shortest of visits to SPL will make abundantly clear, Scotland's contribution to the art is scarcely an inconsiderable one.

Opposite the Royal Mile Primary School (are the railings for the safety of the pupils or of passers-by?) are two local authority housing developments from the 1960s. These sensitive compromises between low-cost and high-quality accommodation were designed by Sir Basil Spence in a style which pays a great deal more respect to historic context than other postmodern abominations of the Mile.

Squashed somewhat awkwardly between the Spence flats is the Canongate manse of **Reid's Court** (N29). The building dates from the 17th century activities of coach-maker James Reid, who also ran a coaching inn here. In the 18th century the building enjoyed a brief relationship with the Canongate Kirk by serving as the minister's home, but by the 19th century had fallen into disrepair. A thorough restoration in 1958 returned the manse to the kirk, and the minister to the manse.

Onwards and downwards – in gradient and, it has to be said, somewhat in interest too, unless fairly limp exploitations of local historical characters at Clarinda's Tea Room and Jenny Ha's Tavern succeed in luring you away from authenticity. On the left, the expansive, whitewashed complex of Whitefoord House has since 1960 provided welcome comfort to Scottish veterans.

A well, dated 1817, is situated just beyond an intriguing little shop specialising in playing cards and opposite

Whitefoord House. Surprisingly, this source of Adam's wine also provided a centre for much racketeering. Water carriers used to hang around such fountains, and because they charged for delivery to residents, were more often than not energetically engaged in fending off rival merchants. Privatised water schemes today ought to be reminded of this illustrative little historical precedent.

Behind the well, **Queensberry House** (s29) looms large. This building now forms an annex to the controversial site of the new Scottish Parliament building. In the early 18th century, a ghastly incident occurred here. The 2nd Duke of Queensberry (1662-1711) was instrumental in pushing through the Act of Union with England in 1707, and is not exactly a well-loved politician as a consequence. His devotion to the bill – not connected in any way, of course, with his acceptance of a bribe of £12,325 – was such that he ventured out one evening with a few supporters to canvass for more signatures, leaving his house empty but for his mentally disturbed eldest son, Lord Drumlanrig, and a kitchen boy. Upon returning home, the Duke's party discovered the lunatic lord roasting the murdered servant on a spit over the kitchen range.

The horror of the event is well documented in local history. On account of diminished responsibility, and with the added advantage of aristocratic blood, the miserable lord was no doubt immune from prosecution. Moralists and nationalists are tempted by the interpretation of divine retribution for the father's cynical ties with the parcel of rogues who were bought and sold for English gold, though the flaw in this account is surely the idiot boy's choice of victim.

Before crossing the Canongate to White Horse Close, however, pause at a radiation of cobbles marking the erstwhile location of the **Girth Cross** (N31), another venue for proclamations and mutilations.

It was here, on 5 July 1600, that the unhappy Lady Warriston met her death from the infamous Maiden for murdering her husband. Although the execution took place at 4 am, a vast crowd had assembled to witness the spectacle. According to eyewitnesses, Lady Warriston 'died very patiently', submitting 'sweetly and graciously' to her executioner's directions. One observer was moved by her dignity and bravery to declare that she was 'ravished with a higher spirit than man's or woman's'. She was twenty-one years old.

Restored in 1965, the date on the building on the north side – 1623 – places the magnificent **White Horse Close** (N30) firmly in the 17th century school of vernacular design. The dwelling furthest distant was the original White Horse Inn, a notoriously dodgy lodging house with a captive market from wide-eyed travellers entering the city by coach from Newcastle or London. After a bum-numbing journey of several days, this coaching stage must have appeared deceptively ingenuous.

During the 1745 Rebellion, the Jacobite commanders commandeered the inn as their Edinburgh headquarters: not a good omen for a doomed and desperate enterprise. The high-heid-yin Bonnie Prince Charlie, of course, bagged somewhat more illustrious quarters just over the road, as he needed somewhere big enough for the series of fashionable parties that would appear to have been the sum total of his contribution to finalising military strategy for the campaign.

We follow him now across the roundabout, down the Abbey Strand, to the Palace of Holyroodhouse, to see what all the fuss was about.

CHAPTER 6

Malice at the Palace

HERE AT LAST IS THE dainty tail of the **Palace of Holyroodhouse** (E1), and the end of the fishbone. As most of Edinburgh for much of its life stank like a bucket of long-dead herring, the metaphor is not merely apposite in an architectural sense. The end of a journey tracing history's skeleton also marks in many senses the completion of a circle, as well as a fairly straight line. Like the Castle, Holyrood Palace is another royal domain, and requires parting with cash to gain access. A full history of the Palace is likewise beyond the remit of this book, which will single out some salient features both conventional and eccentric. The interested reader is directed to an equal plethora of specialised publications, or to the nearest guide.

Before entering, do examine your shoes. Not because admittance is denied to those with an excess of Edinburgh dogs' dos thereon, but rather because you may well be standing on, or near, an important section of the entrance way, signified by the letters S for sanctuary. The letters, on the roadway at the start of the Abbey Strand, mark an old boundary within which refugees and runaways could find asylum. This was requested of the Holyrood Abbot, forerunner of the post-Reformation Bailie, who reserved the right to grant or refuse admission, depending on his mood, quantity of claret imbibed, or the colour of your eyes.

Successful applicants would find themselves within an open prison-like regime, safe from those queuing up outside with cudgels, warrants or rubber cheques. The voluntary incarcerees, furthermore, were permitted 24 hours' safe passage to the outside world every Saturday (disguises not provided), which privilege many chose to enjoy in the Canongate howffs. Although predominantly a medieval custom, sanctuary could be applied for until 1880, and in the latter years of the practice was requested by some eminent individuals. Financially embarrassed doctors and lawyers were frequent customers, and the odd French prince in exile: the eventual Charles x spent his wilderness years within the safe precincts of the Palace.

The device of a small stag with a crucifix between its antlers which embellishes the Edwardian gateway symbol-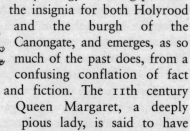ises the ancient origins of this haven, and its etymology. The stag provides the insignia for both Holyrood and the burgh of the Canongate, and emerges, as so much of the past does, from a confusing conflation of fact and fiction. The 11th century Queen Margaret, a deeply pious lady, is said to have acquired a relic of the Cross which she fashioned into a miniature crucifix. After her death the icon passed to her son King David, and remained with him at all times.

During one of his regular hunting expeditions around the then inhospitable royal parks of Arthur's Seat, the King was thrown from his horse and lay injured and helpless on the ground. A huge stag chanced upon the prostrate monarch, and was on the point of airing its grievances on the subject of bloodsports by turning the royal personage into a kebab when the King brandished the crucifix, at the sight of which the stag elected to flee in an attack of vampire-like submission to a superior power. Young David vowed

to honour his miraculous deliverance through divine intervention, founding the Abbey of the Holy Rood (Cross) in
1128.

The seductive sheen of myth decorates much of the history marshalled within these gates. An inspection of the
grounds immediately left of the point of entry reveals, firstly,
a statue of Edward VII, and secondly, the distant Hansel and
Gretel prettiness of Queen Mary's Bath House. Her
Highness is purported to have bathed in claret here, a habit
resisted by her descendants, owing to the very public
scrutiny of such ablutions – bubble-bath or Bolinger –
facilitated by the proximity of the No. 35 corporation bus
route. On a similar note, Harry Gamley's interpretation of
Edward VII tends towards idealisation, since the sculptor
chose to model his own physique in preference to the less
than heroic corpulence and bandy-legs of his subject.

Fortunately, the fountain in the centre of the courtyard
bucks the trend towards an invented past. This is a faithful
Victorian reproduction of an original at Linlithgow Palace,
though it is dry except throughout the Queen's annual
week of residence. Rumours that it spouts Perrier water for
seven days have never been authenticated. At least the
fountain's inoperative condition permits full examination
of its host of decorative characters. Here is David Rizzio
playing his flute; Queen Mary with a broken arm (accident, not design); and a curious three-headed monster in
honour of Britain's last three Prime Ministers. The figures
were designed by none other than the father of the father
of Sherlock Holmes, Sir Arthur Conan Doyle (whose affil-
iations with Edinburgh are, incidentally, fascinating). Was
it foresight or premonition which led Conan Doyle Snr to
include an angular figure sporting a looking-glass and
deerstalker?

Nearing the Palace itself, it is easy to appreciate how this Renaissance grandeur attracts its half million annual pilgrims. The oldest surviving portion is the north-west tower, constructed during 1500-13 at the behest of King James IV. His royal residence was a fitting reflection of Scotland's burgeoning Renaissance culture in a period of short-lived stability and peace, ensured, it was believed, by the Royal marriage between James and the English princess Mary Tudor. Henry VIII of England thought otherwise, and the massacre of Flodden Field in 1513 crushed the flower of a nation.

James V continued to build upon his father's plans for the Palace, but by the time James VI had forsaken the Scottish throne following the Union of the Crowns in 1603 and left a cultural and political vacuum in the capital, a long period of neglect and disrepair for Holyrood had begun. It was the republican Oliver Cromwell, Governor of Scotland, who surprisingly began renovations, though as his work was pulled down a few years later, his artistic tastes were clearly not on a par with his political skills.

It was during the reign of Charles II that the Palace acquired the form seen today. The services of architect Sir William Bruce and master mason Robert Mylne (who built Milne's Court) were enlisted to create the Italianate courtyard quadrangle with arcaded loggia. Internally, the apartments were lavishly decorated with wooden panelling and ornate plasterwork. Upon entry to the Palace, students of fine art will find much to occupy them in almost every room. Almost everybody else will target the apartments of Mary Queen of Scots with the singularity of purpose, speed and accuracy of heat-seeking missiles.

One hopes that Mary was luckier in cards than she was in love, or in choosing husbands. Her reign constituted, more or less, a disastrous and deadly interplay of religious, political and emotional misalliances fomented by one of the most turbulent periods in Scotland's history. Only one episode from the life of a woman now excessively institutionalised and romanticised as *the* definitive Scottish tragic heroine will be given here – though it is probably the most celebrated.

Mary's second husband Lord Darnley had fallen out with marriage, and his bride, within a few months of the wedding, leaving both to play a field overpopulated with predators. Mary inclined to her young Italian secretary David Rizzio as an undoubted confidant, and, according to some sources, a possible lover. Mad with jealousy, Darnley and his followers soon organised Rizzio's callous murder. On the evening of 9 March 1566, Darnley and a band of thugs burst into Mary's private chambers, dragged the screaming Rizzio from her protection, and stabbed him fifty-six times. Today the scene is marked by a plaque on the floor where the butchered body fell, and – for the gullible – bloodstains in the woodwork. At the time of the murder, Mary was six months pregnant. Theories concerning the paternity – and identity – of the baby far outnumber the punctures poor Rizzio received, and will doubtless continue to fuel the MQS industry for a further generation.

The Long Gallery and its famous portrait collection offer some welcome relief. All eighty-nine of the portraits are the work of the Dutch artist Jacob de Witt, who was commissioned in 1684 by Charles II to record for posterity the likenesses of Scotland's lengthy backlist of monarchs. Unfortunately de Witt was not able to avail himself of much in the way of source material, beyond a few rusty trinkets. At £120 a year, though, his creativity was so encouraged that he set about inventing from scratch the visages of at least thirty monarchs, and heavily doctoring the rest. The patrician nose of Charles II provided the model for all his descendants.

This mimicry may have flattered Charles II, but it has offended many other historical and nationalist purists, and in the 1930s proposals were made to remove the family album on the grounds that the paintings were devoid of artistic or historic interest. It is a difficult argument to justify: however confected de Witt's faces are, their production was undeniably conditioned by a particular historical moment, and are consequently as 'historical' as any Old Master. Censorship might prove a dangerous precedent in a place like Holyrood. Dismantle one myth, and others might collapse with it, like a house of cards.

Finally, historians and philosophers who wish to contemplate the imponderable paradoxes of preserving the past will find the ruins of the **Abbey of Holyrood** (E2) provide the most fitting ambience here, or anywhere in Edinburgh for that matter.

In 1688, the Edinburgh mob – on hearing the news of the invasion of William of Orange, and the flight of James VII – pulled the Abbey to pieces, finally releasing this victim of centuries of sacking, bombardment and looting from its tragic vulnerability to armies and war. The multiple arches and rich carvings of the west doorway are stunning vestiges of its past glory. Amidst the ruined choirs in 1829, the composer Mendelssohn found the inspiration for his Scottish symphony. It is a fitting reminder that the trauma and brutishness of the Scottish past, traceable in every step taken down Edinburgh's Royal Mile, is also the raw material of this nation's astonishing wealth of cultural achievement.

Tailpiece

AS DUSK – OR DUST – settles on a review of the Royal Mile which has hopefully been incisive, it is worth rehearsing a few of the themes and issues which have proved unavoidable over the course of the last 1,866 yards. It has been a journey across 16,695 cobblestones, an equal length of tartan plaid, five postboxes, three public toilets, and no nuclear power-stations – yet. Gift emporiums have greatly outnumbered grocers. The reader will have to form independent conclusions concerning the ratio of fact to myth from the extensive evidence provided.

The conflicting interests of an expanding tourist industry and a dwindling residential base place the Royal Mile at a very different kind of crossroads. Is further Disneyfication of this immense historical monument into a fossilised theme-park imminent? Can the balance between preservation and a vibrant urban tradition be maintained, in the ways in which Patrick Geddes proved it to be possible?

Planners are advised to note that while fast cash spews from short-term tourist-led provision, the past upon which tourism feeds is an absolutely non-renewable resource. Commercialisa-tion and modernisation threaten to deface, if not destroy, that past by tearing the heart from this wonderful mile-long living monument.

A Royal Mile without a heart would deprive a nation of its soul.

Glossary

NEWCOMERS TO SCOTTISH CULTURE may find some of the nomenclature pertaining to architecture, the law and language unfamiliar.

Here is a brief guide to the terms most likely to cause confusion.

Clachan   hamlet or village

Close   courtyard or passageway giving access to a number of buildings

Howff   tavern

Land   any property or tenement capable of being inherited

Mercat   market – Mercat Crosses were erected in Scottish burghs as the focus of market activity and local ceremony

Pend   open-ended passage through a building on ground level

Tolbooth   tax office containing a burgh council chamber and prison

Wig   wig

Wynd   narrow lane or alley, often running into a main street

Some other books published by **LUATH** PRESS

Grave Robbers

Robin Mitchell

ISBN 0 946487 72 3 PBK £7.95

After years of sleeping peacefully, the deceased dignitaries of Old Edinburgh are about to get a nasty surprise...

Grave-digger and funeral enthusiast Cameron Carter lives a relatively quiet life. Until a misplaced shovel cracks open a coffin lid and reveals a hidden fortune, that is. Nearly one hundred and seventy years after the trial of Scotland's notorious body snatchers, William Burke and William Hare, the ancient trade of grave robbing returns to the town's cemeteries.

Forming an unholy union with small time crook, Adam, Cameron is drawn into a web of crime that involves a bogus American Scholars' Society, chocolate chip ice cream and Steve McQueen. Their sacrilegious scheming doesn't go quite to plan, however, and events begin to spiral dangerously beyond Cameron the answers will be exhumed.

Will our hero pull the tour guide of his dreams?

Will his partner in crime ever shift those microwaves?

Is there an afterlife?

In Robin Mitchell's rude and darkly comic debut novel, all the answers will be exhumed.

'Good, unclean macabre fun from Robin Mitchell...'
IAN RANKIN

Edinburgh and Leith Pub Guide

Stuart McHardy

ISBN 0 946487 80 4 PBK £4.95

You might be in Edinburgh to explore the closes and wynds of one of Europe's most beautiful cities, to sample the finest Scotch whiskies and to discover a rich Celtic heritage of traditional music and story-telling. Or you might be in Leith to get trashed. Either way, this is the guide for you.

With the able assistance of his long time drinking partner, 'the Man from Fife', Stuart McHardy has dragged his tired old frame around over two hundred pubs – all in the name of research, of course. Alongside drinking numerous pints, he has managed to compile enough historical anecdote and practical information to allow any-one with a sturdy liver to follow in his footsteps.

Although Stuart unashamedly gives top marks to his favourite haunts, he rates most highly those pubs that are original, distinctive and cater to the needs of their clientele. Be it domino league or play-station league, pina colada or a pint of heavy, filled foccacia or mince and tatties, Stuart has found a decent pub that does it.

Over 200 pubs

12 pub trails plus maps

Helpful rating system

Brief guide to Scottish beers and whiskies

'The Man from Fife's wry take on each pub

Discover the answers to such essential questions as:

Which pubs are recommended by whisky wholesalers for sampling?

Where can you find a pub that has links with Bonnie Prince Charlie and Mary Queen of Scots?

Which pub serves kangaroo burgers?

Where can you go for a drop of mead in Edinburgh?

Which pub has a toy crocodile in pride of place behind the bar?

How has Stuart survived all these years?

Long familiar with Edinburgh and Leith's drinking dens, watering holes, shebeens and dens of iniquity, Stuart McHardy has penned a bible for the booze connoisseur. Whether you're here for Hogmanay, a Six Nations weekend, the Festival, just one evening or the rest of your life, this is the companion to slip in your pocket or handbag as you venture out in search of the craic.

Reportage Scotland: History in the Making

Louise Yeoman

Foreword by Professor David Stevenson

ISBN 0 946487 61 8 PBK £9.99

Events – both major and minor – as seen and recorded by Scots throughout history.

Which king was murdered in a sewer?

What was Dr Fian's love magic?

Who was the half-roasted abbot?

Which cardinal was salted and put in a barrel?

Why did Lord Kitchener's niece try to blow up Burns's cottage?

The answers can all be found in this eclectic mix covering nearly 2000 years of Scottish history. Historian Louise Yeoman's rummage through the manuscript, book and newspaper archives of the National Library of Scotland has yielded an astonishing range of material from a letter to the king of the Picts to in Mary Queen of Scots' own account of the murder of David Riccio; from the execution of William Wallace to accounts of anti-poll tax actions and the opening of the new Scottish Parliament. The book takes pieces from the original French, Latin, Gaelic and Scots and makes them accessible to the general reader, often for the first time.

The result is compelling reading for anyone interested in the history that has made Scotland what it is today.

'Marvellously illuminating and wonderfully readable' Angus Calder, SCOTLAND ON SUNDAY

'A monumental achievement in drawing together such a rich historical harvest' Chris Holme, THE HERALD

On the Trail of Mary Queen of Scots

J. Keith Cheetham
ISBN 0 946487 50 2 PBK £7.99

Life dealt Mary Queen of Scots love, intrigue, betrayal and tragedy in generous measure.

On the Trail of Mary Queen of Scots traces the major events in the turbulent life of the beautiful, enigmatic queen whose romantic reign and tragic destiny exerts an undimmed fascination over 400 years after her execution.

Places of interest to visit – 99 in Scotland, 35 in England and 29 in France.

One general map and 6 location maps.

Line drawings and illustrations.

Simplified family tree of the royal houses of Tudor and Stuart.

Key sites include:

Linlithgow Palace – Mary's birthplace, now a magnificent ruin

Stirling Castle – where, only nine months old, Mary was crowned Queen of Scotland

Notre Dame Cathedral – where, aged fifteen, she married the future king of France

The Palace of Holyroodhouse – Rizzio, one of Mary's closest advisers, was murdered here and some say his blood still stains the spot where he was stabbed to death

Sheffield Castle – where for fourteen years she languished as prisoner of her cousin, Queen Elizabeth I

Fotheringhay – here Mary finally met her death on the executioner's block.

On the Trail of Mary Queen of Scots is for everyone interested in the life of perhaps the most romantic figure in Scotland's history; a thorough guide to places connected with Mary, it is also a guide to the complexities of her personal and public life.

'In my end is my beginning'
MARY QUEEN OF SCOTS

'...the woman behaves like the Whore of Babylon' JOHN KNOX

On the Trail of William Wallace

David R. Ross

ISBN 0 946487 47 2 PBK £7.99

How close to reality was *Braveheart*?

Where was Wallace actually born?

What was the relationship between Wallace and Bruce?

Are there any surviving eye-witness accounts of Wallace?

How does Wallace influence the psyche of today's Scots?

On the Trail of William Wallace offers a refreshing insight into the life and heritage of the great Scots hero whose proud story is at the very heart of what it means to be Scottish. Not concentrating simply on the hard historical facts of Wallace's life, the book also takes into account the real significance of Wallace and his effect on the ordinary Scot through the ages, manifested in the many sites where his memory is marked. In trying to piece together the jigsaw of the reality of Wallace's life, David Ross weaves a subtle flow of new information with his own observations. His engaging, thoughtful and at times amusing narrative reads with the ease of a historical novel, complete with all the intrigue, treachery and romance required to hold the attention of the casual reader and still entice the more knowledgable historian.

74 places to visit in Scotland and the north of England

One general map and 3 location maps

Stirling and Falkirk battle plans

Wallace's route through London

Chapter on Wallace connections in North America and elsewhere

Reproductions of rarely seen illustrations

On the Trail of William Wallace will be enjoyed by anyone with an interest in Scotland, from the passing tourist to the most fervent nationalist. It is an encyclopaedia-cum-guide book, literally stuffed with fascinating titbits not usually on offer in the conventional history book.

David Ross is organiser of and historical adviser to the Society of William Wallace.

'Historians seem to think all there is to be known about Wallace has already been uncovered. Mr Ross has proved that Wallace studies are in fact in their infancy.' ELSPETH KING, Director the the Stirling Smith Art Museum & Gallery, who annotated and introduced the recent Luath edition of *Blind Harry's Wallace*.

'Better the pen than the sword!'

RANDALL WALLACE, author of *Braveheart*, when asked by David Ross how it felt to be partly responsible for the freedom of a nation following the Devolution Referendum.

On the Trail of Robert Burns

John Cairney

ISBN 0 946487 51 0 PBK £7.99

Is there anything new to say about Robert Burns?

John Cairney says it's time to trash Burns the Brand and come on the trail of the real Robert Burns. He is the best of travelling companions on this convivial, entertaining journey to the heart of the Burns story.

Internationally known as 'the face of Robert Burns', John Cairney believes that the traditional Burns tourist trail urgently needs to find a new direction. In an acting career spanning forty years he has often lived and breathed Robert Burns on stage. *On the Trail of Robert Burns* shows just how well he can get under the skin of a character. This fascinating journey around Scotland is a rediscovery of Scotland's national bard as a flesh and blood genius.

On the Trail of Robert Burns outlines five tours, mainly in Scotland. Key sites include:

Alloway – Burns' birthplace. Tam O' Shanter draws on the witch-stories about Alloway Kirk first heard by Burns in his childhood.

Mossgiel – between 1784 and 1786 in a phenomenal burst of creativity Burns wrote some of his most memorable poems including Holy Willie's Prayer and To a Mouse.

Kilmarnock - the famous Kilmarnock edition of *Poems Chiefly in the Scottish Dialect* published in 1786.

Edinburgh - fame and Clarinda (among others) embraced him. Dumfries - Burns died at the age of 37. The trail ends at the Burns mausoleum in St Michael's churchyard.

'For me an aim I never fash I rhyme for fun' ROBERT BURNS

'My love affair on stage with Burns started in London in 1959. It was consumated on stage at the Traverse Theatre in Edinburgh in 1965 and has continued happily ever since' JOHN CAIRNEY

'The trail is expertly, touchingly and amusingly followed' THE HERALD

Scotland: Myth, Legend and Folklore

Stuart McHardy

ISBN 0 946487 69 3 PBK 7.99

Who were the people who built the megaliths?

What great warriors sleep beneath the Hollow Hills?

Were the early Scottish saints just pagans in disguise?

Was King Arthur really Scottish?

When was Nessie first sighted?

This is a book about Scotland drawn from hundreds, if not thousands of years of storytelling. From the oral traditions of the Scots, Gaelic and Norse speakers of the past, it presents a new picture of who the Scottish are and where they come from. The stories that McHardy recounts may be hilarious, tragic, heroic, frightening or just plain bizzare, but they all provide an insight into a unique tradition of myth, legend and folklore that has marked both the language and landscape of Scotland.

FOLKLORE

The Supernatural Highlands
Francis Thompson
ISBN 0 946487 31 6 PBK £8.99

Tall Tales from an Island
Peter Macnab
ISBN 0 946487 07 3 PBK £8.99

Tales from the North Coast
Alan Temperley
ISBN 0 946487 18 9 PBK £8.99

ON THE TRAIL OF

On the Trail of Robert the Bruce
David R. Ross
ISBN 0 946487 52 9 PBK £7.99

On the Trail of Robert Service
GW Lockhart
ISBN 0 946487 24 3 PBK £7.99

On the Trail of John Muir
Cherry Good
ISBN 0 946487 62 6 PBK £7.99

NEW SCOTLAND

**Scotland - Land and Power
the agenda for land reform**
Andy Wightman
foreword by Lesley Riddoch
ISBN 0 946487 70 7 PBK £5.00

Old Scotland New Scotland
Jeff Fallow
ISBN 0 946487 40 5 PBK £6.99

**Notes from the North
incorporating a Brief History of
the Scots and the English**
Emma Wood
ISBN 0 946487 46 4 PBK £8.99

SOCIAL HISTORY

Shale Voices
Alistair Findlay
foreword by Tam Dalyell MP
ISBN 0 946487 63 4 PBK £10.99
ISBN 0 946487 78 2 HBK £17.99

Crofting Years
Francis Thompson
ISBN 0 946487 06 5 PBK £6.95

A Word for Scotland
Jack Campbell
foreword by Magnus Magnusson
ISBN 0 946487 48 0 PBK £12.99

LUATH GUIDES TO SCOTLAND

Mull and Iona: Highways and Byways
Peter Macnab
ISBN 0 946487 58 8 PBK £4.95

South West Scotland
Tom Atkinson
ISBN 0 946487 04 9 PBK £4.95

The West Highlands: The Lonely Lands
Tom Atkinson
ISBN 0 946487 56 1 PBK £4.95

The Northern Highlands: The Empty Lands
Tom Atkinson
ISBN 0 946487 55 3 PBK £4.95

The North West Highlands: Roads to the Isles
Tom Atkinson
ISBN 0 946487 54 5 PBK £4.95

WALK WITH LUATH

Mountain Days & Bothy Nights
Dave Brown and Ian Mitchell
ISBN 0 946487 15 4 PBK £7.50

The Joy of Hillwalking
Ralph Storer
ISBN 0 946487 28 6 PBK £7.50

Scotland's Mountains before the Mountaineers
Ian Mitchell
ISBN 0 946487 39 1 PBK £9.99

LUATH WALKING GUIDES

Walks in the Cairngorms
Ernest Cross
ISBN 0 946487 09 X PBK £4.95

Short Walks in the Cairngorms
Ernest Cross
ISBN 0 946487 23 5 PBK £4.95

FICTION

The Bannockburn Years
William Scott
ISBN 0 946487 34 0 PBK £7.95

The Great Melnikov
Hugh MacLachlan
ISBN 0 946487 42 1 PBK £7.95

NATURAL SCOTLAND

Wild Scotland: The essential guide to finding the best of natural Scotland
James McCarthy
Photography by Laurie Campbell
ISBN 0 946487 37 5 PBK £7.50

'Nothing but Heather!'
Gerry Cambridge
ISBN 0 946487 49 9 PBK £15.00

**Scotland Land and People
An Inhabited Solitude**
James McCarthy
ISBN 0 946487 57 X PBK £7.99

The Highland Geology Trail
John L Roberts
ISBN 0 946487 36 7 PBK £4.99

Rum: Nature's Island
Magnus Magnusson
ISBN 0 946487 32 4 PBK £7.95

Red Sky at Night
John Barrington
ISBN 0 946487 60 X PBK £8.99

Listen to the Trees
Don MacCaskill
ISBN 0 946487 65 0 PBK £9.99

BIOGRAPHY

Tobermory Teuchter: A first-hand account of life on Mull in the early years of the 20th century
Peter Macnab
ISBN 0 946487 41 3 PBK £7.99

Bare Feet and Tackety Boots
Archie Cameron
ISBN 0 946487 17 0 PBK £7.95

Come Dungeons Dark
John Taylor Caldwell
ISBN 0 946487 19 7 PBK £6.95

MUSIC AND DANCE

Highland Balls and Village Halls
GW Lockhart
ISBN 0 946487 12 X PBK £6.95

Fiddles & Folk: A celebration of the re-emergence of Scotland's musical heritage
GW Lockhart
ISBN 0 946487 38 3 PBK £7.95

SPORT

Over the Top with the Tartan Army (Active Service 1992-97)
Andrew McArthur
ISBN 0 946487 45 6 PBK £7.99

Ski & Snowboard Scotland
Hilary Parke
ISBN 0 946487 35 9 PBK £6.99

Pilgrims in the Rough: St Andrews beyond the 19th hole
Michael Tobert
ISBN 0 946487 74 X PBK £7.99

POETRY

Poems to be read aloud
Collected and with an introduction by Tom Atkinson
ISBN 0 946487 00 6 PBK £5.00

Blind Harry's Wallace
William Hamilton of Gilbertfield introduced by Elspeth King
ISBN 0 946487 43 X HBK £15.00
ISBN 0 946487 33 2 PBK £8.99

Luath Press Limited

committed to publishing well written books worth reading

LUATH PRESS takes its name from Robert Burns, whose little collie Luath (*Gael.*, swift or nimble) tripped up Jean Armour at a wedding and gave him the chance to speak to the woman who was to be his wife and the abiding love of his life. Burns called one of *The Twa Dogs* Luath after Cuchullin's hunting dog in *Ossian's Fingal*. Luath Press grew up in the heart of Burns country, and now resides a few steps up the road from Burns' first lodgings in Edinburgh's Royal Mile. Luath offers you distinctive writing with a hint of unexpected pleasures.

Most UK and US bookshops either carry our books in stock or can order them for you. To order direct from us, please send a £sterling cheque, postal order, international money order or your credit card details (number, address of cardholder and expiry date) to us at the address below. Please add post and packing as follows: UK – £1.00 per delivery address; overseas surface mail – £2.50 per delivery address; overseas airmail – £3.50 for the first book to each delivery address, plus £1.00 for each additional book by airmail to the same address. If your order is a gift, we will happily enclose your card or message at no extra charge.

Luath Press Limited
543/2 Castlehill
The Royal Mile
Edinburgh EH1 2ND
Scotland
Telephone: 0131 225 4326 (24 hours)
Fax: 0131 225 4324
email: gavin.macdougall@luath.co.uk
Website: www.luath.co.uk